"Loren Sandford is a credible seer—a prophet—and has seen into the future. *Visions of the Coming Days* will provoke healthy questions in some and offer enlightening confirmation to many. Awesome days await those who are prepared. Loren Sandford, through this book, will help you prepare."

Patricia King, XP Ministries

"As a healing ministry called to God's leaders to enable them to deal with their wounding, it is refreshing to have a prophetic book direct us to Father's heart. Loren's many stern and direct cautions and warnings, based on current trends in Christiandom, are not to shame us, but to get us back on track to Father's love. His love calls us higher, drawing us into His healing. As we heal, we can drop the defenses of pride, etc., enabling us to repent and seek the Father's heart. Thank you, Loren, for this trumpet call."

Chester and Betsy Kylstra, founders,
Restoring the Foundations Ministries

"As a co-worker and fellow warrior of Loren in both the Western world and eastern Europe, I heartily recommend *Visions of the Coming Days*. His razor-sharp words of warning and rebuke can be startling, but they are tempered by the Father's love for His people in an age of muddled values and lifestyles within the Body of Christ. His words pierce the conscience and drop the plumb line, but he is speaking from a heart longing for redemption and grace. This is a call for examination and accountability of self and the Church in the light of the mercy and truth of our Lord's nature as the Lion and the Lamb. I've witnessed Loren's focus on others and not self in very uncomfortable settings, so I know he is moving forward in personally living out what he writes here. Read with an open heart!"

Dan Slade, international coordinator,
Partners in Harvest Network, Toronto, Canada

VISIONS
OF THE
COMING
DAYS

VISIONS
OF THE
COMING
DAYS

WHAT TO LOOK FOR AND HOW TO PREPARE

R. LOREN SANDFORD

Chosen

a division of Baker Publishing Group
Minneapolis, Minnesota

© 2012 by R. Loren Sandford

Published by Chosen Books
11400 Hampshire Avenue South
Bloomington, Minnesota 55438
www.chosenbooks.com

Chosen Books is a division of
Baker Publishing Group, Grand Rapids, Michigan

Printed in the United States of America

Library of Congress Cataloging-in-Publication Data
Sandford, R. Loren.
    Visions of the coming days : what to look for and how to prepare / R. Loren Sandford.
        p.   cm.
    ISBN 978-0-8007-9530-6 (pbk. : alk. paper)
    1. End of the world. 2. Eschatology. 3. Bible—Prophecies. I. Title.
BT877.S26 2012
236—dc23   2012002134

Scripture quotations are from the New American Standard Bible®, copyright © 1960, 1962, 1963, 1968, 1971, 1972, 1973, 1975, 1977, 1995 by The Lockman Foundation. Used by permission.

The internet addresses, email addresses, and phone numbers in this book are accurate at the time of publication. They are provided as a resource. Baker Publishing Group does not endorse them or vouch for their content or permanence.

Cover design by Lookout Design, Inc.

18 19 20 21 22 23 24   8 7 6 5 4 3 2

CONTENTS

Contents

FOREWORD

I love God's ways, God's power, God's authority and how God acts on our behalf before we even ask. I also love true prophetic words, divine supernatural encounters and dreams from God. It is through these events and other miracles that God confirms His deity. He is constantly displaying His attributes of omniscience, omnipotence, omnipresence, immutability and eternality every day in our lives. Whether we recognize the splendor of His acts or not does not dilute or diminish the fact that He wants us to know Him in a vast panorama of ways.

In the midst of all of heaven's interventions, I believe we are to do as the Bible has instructed us to do: We are to tell of His wonderful deeds and teach them to our children and our children's children. In so doing, all remain in awe of God.

We are also to continue to give God all the glory and take none of that glory upon ourselves. We are not to exaggerate what He has done, diminish what He has said or tell things that He did not do as if He did them. We are to hold clear and strong biblical doctrines, and live those beliefs before mankind. In so doing, we are to be witnesses to others of all God has done and is doing, and give others hope that God will continue to act as He has.

Regrettably this is not happening on a widespread basis today. In fact, we, the Body of Christ, are experiencing less and less relevance to the world we were placed here to influence. As a result we are living in a time when the logic of politicians, the cleverness of pundits, the sermons of pulpiteers and the revelations of prophets are all failing to capture the hearts of the people they are hoping will listen. This should not be true, but it is.

Jesus and the prophets of Scripture prophesied, with alarming accuracy, that a time will come when the humanistic logic of man will lead to the perplexity of nations. That time has arrived. Today's logic, at best, may solve human quandaries in the short term, but it exacerbates those quandaries in the long run. The fruit of this line of thinking is now being harvested, and the perplexity of nations has expanded and become global.

Conversely, especially within the broader charismatic/evangelical Church, there arises an equally anti-logic sentiment of a "nice" God who would never chastise or spank His children. Paralleling this anti-logic paradigm is a mindset in which spiritual experiences become the goal. If left unchecked, this mindset will broaden to become an accepted rule of theology. Thus, in some circles, spiritual experiences are sought more than a deep relationship with God. This experience-oriented atmosphere rapidly leads to a perspective that what happens *to* you is more important than what happens *in* you; when the verbalization of your experience becomes more important than the transformation of your being; and, even more saddening, when your philosophy becomes more important than your theology.

Subtly, almost imperceptibly, the yeast of a philosophical approach to Scripture is rising and a philosophically moralistic perspective of God is taking over. Thus, if God is love, there can be no such place as hell; marriage is seen as a convenience rather than a covenant; sin management is sought more than sin eradication; and even the devil will get saved.

If this continues, you will see an increasing emphasis placed on so-called spiritual feelings and the intellectualization of spiritual realities that attempt to make imagination equal to true supernatural experiences. In other words, if you can imagine it, you have experienced it. I am afraid we have arrived at a crossroads where the Tree of Knowledge of Good and Evil and the Tree of Life have become almost indistinguishable. Sadly, more are climbing the wrong tree and unknowingly getting steeped in the acceptance of New Age thinking as a legitimate means of promoting Christian experience.

If we are not careful, we will find that in our efforts to help the Body of Christ accept the biblical truth of the *charismata* of Scripture, we have lowered the standards for the exercise of those spiritual gifts. It seems we have forgotten the need for integrity and character to be woven into the life of any person who has been given a spiritual gift. Thus, weak and incomplete prophetic words are treated as if they were mature while errant prophecies are left unaddressed. This is already happening. As a result, those with supposed spiritual gifts, rather than creating a new hunger for biblical truths and the supernatural gifts of the Holy Spirit within the Church, have begun to alienate other believers.

If this malaise continues, we will find ourselves in a Church repelled by the new wine God is longing to display, since the old wine tastes good enough.

If mature, pure revelation from God is not released, the profane will take its place, and all too quickly we will find ourselves on a swift spiritual decline. In this decline, apathy will be touted as being peaceful, zeal will be choked out as being troublesome, lethargy will be seen as being compliant, and passion will be seen as rebellion.

Already, in many circles, the term *holy* is seen as a devilish four-letter word, and *righteousness* has become a synonym for *legalism*.

We are rapidly approaching a convergence in which, as Jeremiah wrote, prophets and priests cause people to err through their false dreams and recklessness. There is now increasing evidence that both are becoming epidemic in proportion.

A balance must be struck, a balance of Word and Spirit. In finding that balance, we will once again be able to separate the holy from the profane, the precious from the vile, and the clean from the unclean.

I believe what Loren Sandford has written in *Visions of the Coming Days* is not only a wake-up call toward that end, but it denotes a map on how to view prophecy today in respect to the even more important prophecies and revelatory principles contained in the Bible.

I am sure many who read this book will, at some point, become upset and even angry at Loren for the bold stance he is taking. This book is not a sugar-coated address of a caustic problem. It is tough love mixed with brute reality. Its intent is to stir a rethinking in the hearts and lives of those who are truly hungry for a deeper and fuller relationship with God, and what He has already told us is coming our way.

In some ways it may seem as if Loren is trying to awaken a slumbering Bride with a nuclear warhead; but then the scales of complacency are not easily sloughed off, and when soft words have not worked, more difficult words follow.

May *Visions of the Coming Days* change the way we view not only prophetic events and prophecies of things to come, but our own actions and the way we perceive the Church and its impact on the world in which we live. One way or another, the world is about to change radically. It will never be the same again.

John Paul Jackson, founder and president
Streams Ministries International

INTRODUCTION

Although the title includes the word *visions*, this book includes very few actual visions in the mystical sense. Unlike many other prophetic voices, I receive little revelation by means of dream or vision. My gift flows more from simple intimacy with God. For this reason do not expect pages filled with symbolic imagery, mystical experiences, reports of open visions or translations to heaven, but rather some very direct statements from the heart of the Father concerning the days to come.

More important, I speak as a pastor whom many have come to regard as a prophet. Whatever names people choose to call me, however, the role of a pastor who loves people and longs to see them live well in the Lord Jesus Christ comes first. For this reason I cannot merely prophesy events to come without teaching in relation to them and, thus, preparing the Body of Christ in clear and practical ways to meet them. I have, therefore, devoted major portions of this book to undergirding the prophetic word with teaching both to explain coming events and to prepare God's people to meet them. To the best of my ability, I have rooted this teaching in Scripture and in scriptural principles.

Were I to inspire too much fear in the believers who read these words, I would certainly fail the Lord's intention to equip His people. For this reason I have worked to balance negative predictions with valid promises of glory and hope. Our God has not given us a spirit of fear. According to the apostle John, God's perfect love casts out fear (see 1 John 4:18).

According to Jeremiah 1:10, a primary function of prophetic ministry is to tear down that which is not of God and to build up what is. It plucks up what God did not plant and plants those things that truly come from Him. For this reason, I have not limited this book to predictions, but have prophetically confronted pollutions, foreign influences and other issues that have crept into the Body of Christ. In most cases, these connect directly with events to come. Dealing in a godly way with these pollutions and influences forms an essential part of the Church's preparation for the days to come.

I have repeated a number of prophecies, prophetic confrontations and related issues a number of times throughout the book in order to highlight them in various contexts. My reason for doing so is that it will be crucial to connect the dots in days to come, and to understand clearly how core issues affect a variety of circumstances. Much of the prophetic content of this book presents an understanding of the signs of the times and forms an interwoven tapestry of understanding and proposed action.

I make no claim to absolute accuracy. Let the reader judge my level of accuracy in light of what actually transpires in the years to come. Since we are fresh out of Isaiahs and Jeremiahs, I think it unreasonable for the Body of Christ to expect the level of accuracy from modern-day prophetic people that those giants of the faith exhibited. I expect to be tested as 1 Corinthians 14:29 commands. I believe, however, that we who prophesy must be substantially accurate—much as Agabus was substantially accurate, but not 100 percent, in prophesying that Paul would be arrested and bound by the Jews if he went to Jerusalem. In reality, the Romans, not the Jews, arrested and bound him. My record of accuracy has been strong, but if I prove to be wrong in more than minor issues as judged by the fulfillment of my words—or lack thereof—I promise to acknowledge my error quickly and beg forgiveness of the Lord's people. Integrity demands this.

Because I believe the spirit of the words I deliver to be just as important as the content of the words themselves, I consider it important for the reader to understand who I am and where I come from. The Father's heart must infuse the whole. The first section, three chapters in length, therefore, contains more personal testimony and teaching than prophetic content, although both are included. These three chapters provide an essential foundation for fully understanding what comes later.

PART **I**

SETTING
THE TONE

1

HAVING GOD'S HEART

In recent years many in the Body of Christ have developed a strong vertical awareness, an often off-balance emphasis on the supernatural, and have become comfortable with stories of the miraculous, mysterious spiritual experiences and supernatural events. In some circles dreams, visions and angelic encounters have become common topics of conversation. Numbers of us have been schooled in marketplace ministry and have become accustomed to participating in and hearing about signs and wonders performed in public places. This has ignited hunger for more of the same and, among average folk, a desire to move higher in such things.

In the midst of this, however, I sense a different kind of hunger growing among believers. Most have not been able to articulate it beyond expressing an inner ache for something more. Vertical awareness and connection with the Holy Spirit for supernatural living can only be good, but I see a growing longing for a kind of growth that goes the other way, not vertically, but into the depths of the heart. Although the content of this chapter is more an introduction to who I am than an exposition of the prophecies I will set forth later, I predict a growing shift in the Body of Christ from a consuming focus on supernatural experiences to a deeper and more settled intimacy with God.

Growing Up in Renewal

I grew up in the charismatic renewal when the Holy Spirit impacted many thousands of people in dead mainline denominational churches. For many who had never really experienced Him before, God came alive. For my family it all began in 1958 when I was seven years old. Since then I have witnessed and lived through wave after wave of the Holy Spirit as He impacted different segments of the Body of Christ in similar ways, yet with varied emphases as each one fed its unique contribution into the whole.

Some focused on experiencing baptism with the Spirit and speaking in tongues. In other streams passion for divine physical healing grew, while inner healing consumed the attention of others. I can think of at least two waves of prophetic ministry that have come and gone in my lifetime. Still another is currently under way. Through the years, evangelism came in pulses under different headings like "power evangelism," "prophetic evangelism," "friendship evangelism" and others.

Sooner or later each of these movements succumbed to a growing focus on self and personal blessing—the pursuit of personal experiences of God in an obsessively self-centered culture—which makes for a straight line to depression. God built us not for self-focus, but to reflect His nature in selfless sacrifice for others in love. As a violation of our true selves, therefore, self-focus can ultimately produce no other outcome than loss of hope, relational destruction and emotional misery. Driven by the culture around us, the cry became, "Heal *me*! Prophesy over *me*! Baptize *me* in the Spirit! Give *me* revelatory dreams!" We flocked to conferences to learn how to experience divine dreams and how to interpret them. Many sought out books on how to initiate angelic encounters or open heavenly portals. We studied methods for ministering and receiving healing. Mostly these things were good, but the way we used them often was not.

In most renewal circles in which I move, we have become fascinated by manifestations of the Spirit, spiritual trances and things like orbs that show up in digital pictures (which, based on my own experimentation, I am convinced are just dust particles). Prophetic people in particular have spoken openly and too often of dramatic divine encounters, translations to heaven, angelic appearances and visions. Thousands have, therefore, developed a longing for these same experiences until that longing has become the focus of their spirituality. Prophetic ministry has suffered for it.

My Own Prophetic Calling

Through it all, although I have not wanted to be, I have remained a frustratingly sane and sober man. It has seemed as though everyone else at the party got to drink while I remained the designated driver. Someone had to stay sober and it was always me. Why could it not be someone else from time to time?

As I have so often done since the Holy Spirit impacted my family all those years ago, I found myself at some point in 2009 whining to God about this. Why have I been denied the kinds of experiences so many others in the River of the Spirit so often claim to experience? I never fall under the power. Holy laughter has eluded me. I do laugh, joyously, but I laugh at those who laugh, as opposed to laughing as one of them. Other prophetic people I associate with report strange and marvelous spiritual experiences like being translated to heaven or being transported across great distances in impossibly short periods of time. In his dreams my father used to meet with a friend from the other side of the country who was having the same dreams at the same times. Other prophetic people I have known over the years tell of open visions in which they receive great revelations.

I do twitch a bit sometimes when the Spirit moves, and I have started saying *shabba* involuntarily when the Holy Spirit impacts me, but I manifest little else. Heidi Baker of Iris Ministries in Mozambique started that one in me and I told myself I would never manifest anything like that, but there it is, the Lord's sense of humor. Granted, I have experienced three angelic appearances, two in dreams when God sent messages of guidance, and one in a waking state that resulted in a physical healing, but these were spread over almost twenty years. Not enough for me. While everyone else gets drunk in the Spirit, I remain the sober one, and I like it not!

Even so, people in ever-increasing circles relate to me as a reliable prophetic voice. Absent all the weirdness so many others experience as the vehicle of their prophetic revelation, I asked the Lord, "Why do I so often seem to get it right when so many who have the mystical experiences seem often to get it wrong?" What I am about to share with you forms the basis for the prophecies included in this book. It explains the source of any and all revelation I have received concerning the days to come.

The Father's Heart

In 1988, Bob Jones called me aside at a conference to give me a prophetic word and declared, "I have my little dreams and visions, but you're a Nathan prophet. You just know things." This has been true over the years. I have simply known things that God was doing, or not doing—prophetic things He wanted me to know—but I have never really known why or how I knew.

22

I found myself one day whining to the Lord for the umpteenth time concerning my lack of weird mystical experiences when He suddenly spoke into my spirit very gently and clearly, *Yes, but you have My heart*. Something deep in me broke, tears filled my eyes and I have been pondering the meaning of it ever since.

Whatever prophetic accuracy I have demonstrated has never flowed from psychic abilities, mystical experiences or floods of dreams and visions, but from knowing and understanding the heart of God at some level. I could not tell you clearly how I know but I seem to understand instinctively the moving of His heart. To know and live the Father's heart has been my consuming passion, and in many ways I have surrendered every other pursuit. When God spoke to me about having His heart I realized that He has been drawing me in that direction all my life, even when I have not been consciously aware of it.

A foundational truth for all genuine prophetic ministry is this: *If you have God's heart then you know what God knows*. All consistently accurate prophecy and all consistently effective ministry of any kind flows from this fountainhead.

The Heart of God in Revival

My sense of revival history tells me that most revivals have died and faded away because they had the presence of God, the power of God and the manifestations of the Spirit, but they did not have the heart of the Father, or they had it and then lost it when they began to hunger after the wrong things. We can experience flashes of revival, manifestations, healings and prophetic ministry, and some churches can spring up to significant numbers when God sends these things, but if we fail to carry His heart, it will all be temporary.

Are you a prophetic person? Stop being obsessed with dreams, visions, out-of-body experiences and angelic appearances. These things will happen from time to time as God Himself deems them necessary and moves to initiate them, but as a focus of our attention they lead us in the wrong direction. The focus of our hunger must ever remain on the Father's heart. If we speak for Him, we must speak from His heart, in the Spirit of His heart and in a way that manifests His nature.

Pharisees

The Pharisees in Jesus' day immersed themselves in Scripture and practiced strict godly morality. No adultery. No theft. No open sins. They honored the Sabbath and carefully tithed 10 percent of all the money they made and all the produce they grew. Three times a day at the prescribed hours they prayed faithfully and offered all the required sacrifices. No generation before them had worked harder than they to obey the demands of the Law as they interpreted and applied them. In addition to all this, God had entrusted them with stewardship of the prophetic word as delivered through the prophets.

In spite of all this apparent holiness, Jesus found them insufferable. Why? Because they had failed to understand God's heart and, in that failure, they misinterpreted and misapplied everything they knew. You can have God's Word in Scripture, and even receive the "now" revelation of what God will do in the coming days, but His Word will not yield its benefit; you will never truly understand its meaning and you will fail to speak in His Spirit unless you have His heart. "Why do you not understand what I am saying? It is because you cannot hear My word. You are of your father the devil" (John 8:43–44). The Pharisees had become a people of the Word, but they failed to apprehend God's heart embedded in His Word. Believing that they valued Scripture, they actually listened to demons.

In the prophetic words recorded in this book, I desire to speak from the Father's heart. For much of my life, I failed in that regard. Yes, I have grown, but the journey continues.

Confessions of "Self"

I share the following personal confessions regarding my own journey not just so that you will know who I am, but in hopes that others who would move in the prophetic might recognize themselves and seek a greater level of wholeness. I am convinced that we have had little good prophecy over the years, and I know that a time approaches, and now is, when good prophecy will be vital to the Church. Bear with me, therefore, and if my story helps you either to hear my words in later chapters or to grow in your own sense of the prophetic, then I will be a happy man.

You could not have found a more self-focused young man than I in my 20s and early 30s. For instance, when my wife, Beth, and I got married in 1972, her grandfather would slip her little love gifts of money. In my selfishness I always found a way to talk her out of it and convince her to spend that money on some toy or bit of stereo equipment that I wanted, rationalizing it by saying, "It's for *us*!" In my selfishness I stole her blessings. I did this even while leading young people to the Lord and while seeing people healed and transformed when I prayed for them. I did this while ministering in the church as a pastor dedicated to serving God and His people.

I even allowed foolishness and self-focus to endanger my young family. Having always had a fascination with English sports cars, in 1973 I bought a 1967 Austin Healey Sprite. To say that it needed work would be to label Niagara Falls a country creek, but I had stars in my eyes that blinded me to the truth.

That summer my wife and I took a trip from Sacramento, California, where I served as the youth pastor at Hope UMC, to north Idaho to visit family. Convincing myself that the Austin Healey would be more reliable and economical than our perfectly serviceable four-door 1964 Plymouth Valiant with plenty of room—I really just wanted to drive the Austin Healey and be cool—I crammed my pregnant wife, two babies, my guitar and all our clothing into that tiny ragtop two-seater. Top down with the wind in my hair, I was in heaven, oblivious to my wife's discomfort as our younger child danced on her swelling tummy. I then reaped what I had sown when the car broke down in the middle of the night miles from nowhere. God miraculously rescued us and, humbled, I learned a valuable lesson.

The Source of My Problem

In all this I suffered from a root of insecurity that sprang out of much rejection growing up. Behind most arrogance lies a heart wounded in this way.

I grew up with parents who pioneered in the charismatic renewal, in prophetic ministry and in inner healing. In those days these things were new and unknown in much of the Christian world. Historically, the Body of Christ has seldom received new revelations with grace and faith, and my parents' revelations were no exception. What would later be widely accepted drew vicious persecution in the early days. For my parents and for us as children it was much like growing up on a battlefield caught in the cross fire. It hurt, and badly.

People tend to react to pain by developing defense mechanisms. Ours was a form of arrogance. We told ourselves that we Sandfords had the truth and that our persecutors were just "sick." We knew the deep things of the Spirit while our enemies just failed to get it. To make matters worse, I was one of those children who not only took the shots for his parents, but suffered rejection in his own right from peers at school.

All of this led to ambition and arrogance in my adult life as a defense against the pain. Recognition became important to me and I developed a hunger for the platform at meetings. At the same time I suffered tremendous fear that if actually granted the platform I would be rejected or that I would fail.

In the youthful arrogance that concealed my insecurity, I thought I knew more than anybody else because I was, after all, a Sandford, son of international leaders in the charismatic renewal, pioneers in prophetic ministry and inner healing. Can you hear the angels singing through my halo? I used to sit in the back row at conferences and criticize the worship leader in my heart. *I could do better than that! He just doesn't get it.* I judged their musicianship, choice of songs and even the mix from the sound system. I aimed the same arrows at speakers and teachers. In retrospect, I cry, "Gag me with a spoon!"

This describes a great many prophetic wannabes I have known through the years. Much bad prophecy flows from the fountain-head of this kind of arrogance, which is really just compensation for the root of insecurity and rejection.

Pursuing the Heart of Jesus

Early on, even in the midst of all this brokenness, I knew enough to determine that I wanted to become like Jesus, no matter what that might cost. Although I stood a lot farther from that goal than I thought, it remained my heart's desire. In His incredible love, God responded by sending me into situations designed to break, crush and even humiliate me in order to expose my weakness so that it could be transformed into something He could use. I had it coming. A 27-year dark night of the soul ensued, but that is another story. Through it all, the heart of the Father remained my goal.

At some point during the 1980s I found myself yet again complaining to God about not getting blasted by the Spirit with overwhelming spiritual experiences as so many others had. I decided whining was a legitimate form of prayer—read the psalms—and so in response to my cries the Lord asked me a question: *Which would you rather have? Foolish power or powerful wisdom?*

Because I had read Solomon's reply to a similar question, I knew how to respond. I therefore answered correctly, but had yet to learn that knowledge can come from study but real wisdom comes only from suffering. Suffering came. Firsthand, I learned the meaning of Ecclesiastes 7:2–4,

> It is better to go to a house of mourning than to go to a house of feasting, because that is the end of every man, and the living takes it to heart. Sorrow is better than laughter, for when a face is sad a heart may be happy. The mind of the wise is in the house of mourning, while the mind of fools is in the house of pleasure.

I was sick of being the cause of anyone's pain, fed up with my arrogance and weary of offending anyone unnecessarily. Fear had worn me out and I was ready to be done with it. I could no longer live with insecurity and the need to be recognized as someone important. Most of all, I was tired of misrepresenting God, even if unintentionally. I longed to see those ugly character flaws written out of my life and I longed for peace. That much I understood, but God knew the truth, that I hungered after His heart—His selfless, loving, gentle, humble heart.

When He told me, therefore, not so long ago, *Yes, but you have My heart*, something broke inside of me and the tears began to flow. A sweeter, more beautiful thing could not have been spoken by my Father. Brokenness is a wonderful state of being. Although I am acutely aware of how far I have yet to go and always will be, this word from God ministered to my wounded soul.

I share this personal testimony by way of saying that I am not impressed with myself or any revelation God may grant me. I am just a pastor from Denver, an ordinary man with all the frailties and self-doubts that come with the human condition. Neither am I an Isaiah or a Jeremiah. Neither I nor anyone else will ever achieve their level of accuracy and authority. I only know that I must speak what I believe the Father gives me. I share all this also by way of saying that these prophetic words come not from mystical dreams and visions but from what I know to be the heart of God. I pray that the words of this book carry the Father's heart, even as I say many things difficult for some to hear.

No More Train Wrecks

"The sacrifices of God are a broken spirit; a broken and a contrite heart, O God, You will not despise" (Psalm 51:17). Giftedness without brokenness becomes hurtfulness. How often have we seen this principle played out as leader after prominent leader has fallen morally? I could not begin to tell all the stories of wounding by abusive leaders in churches and ministries all over the world that hurting people have poured out to me.

Several years ago, in a moment of frustration over our church's lack of growth, I was again practicing my most holy form of prayer—whining! It seemed the Lord allowed my staff and me no degree of compromise or character flaw without exposing it and forcing us to deal with it. Meanwhile, He kept our numbers small and refused to grant us the church growth we worked so hard to produce. At the same time, I knew firsthand the sins and abuses perpetrated by leaders of some of the mega-churches with which I had become familiar. Protesting the unfairness of it all, I cried out to God, "Why do You bless those guys when I know what they're doing while You hold us back and refuse to allow us any slack at all when we're not nearly so guilty?"

I have never forgotten the answer: *My people can't afford any more train wrecks.* I came to see that the glory sent to bless us becomes a weight and a pressure that can destroy us as it forces open whatever cracks exist in the foundation of our character, revealing our unhealed defects. As a result, many people can be badly hurt.

Apparently unable to face himself, King Saul harbored a deep root of insecurity that never healed. In 1 Samuel 9:21, as Samuel called him to be anointed king, he protested, "Am I not a Benjamite, of the smallest of the tribes of Israel, and my family the least of all the families of the tribe of Benjamin? Why then do you speak to me in this way?" This character flaw led Saul to fail in obedience on more than one occasion and to feel so threatened by David's success as a leader and warrior that it broke his mind. In his insanity he sought to kill the very man who wished only to bless him.

In the New Testament Judas Iscariot shared in the ministry of the Kingdom of God alongside the other disciples, going out with the eleven to perform signs and wonders and proclaim the Gospel of the Kingdom. When hidden character flaws have not been faced, however, the glory sent to bless becomes a destructive pressure. Judas betrayed to death the very One he loved.

In modern times many of us have grieved over the failure of the Lakeland Revival. We have seen the fall of more leaders of mega-churches and international ministries than I care to count. Some failed sexually. Others saw their marriages break up. Still others have been under investigation for financial abuses. One ministry rule I live by might be stated this way: "Success is always and in every case toxic." This does not mean that we must avoid success. Because He receives no glory from our lack and because He loves us beyond understanding, God longs for us to succeed. Problems arise, however, when the foundation in our character cannot bear the weight of the glory God sends.

Desperately, I long to be whole. I pray for God to come in revival, but I do not want to seek wholeness *so that* God will come. I want to be whole *because* God is coming. I want to be ready to safely bear the weight of glory already unfolding. I want to speak the prophetic word with clarity and wholeness.

Hear, therefore, the prophetic word: We are a long way from the end of seeing such failures exposed. Unfortunately, in the days to come, as the Great Apostasy gains momentum, we will see the Church becoming more and more accepting of such moral failures and less and less willing to enforce real accountability. As a result we will struggle with a growing loss of credibility in the eyes of the world, and even within certain segments of the Church.

Focus on the Cross

"And when I came to you, brethren, I did not come with superiority of speech or of wisdom, proclaiming to you the testimony of God. For I determined to know nothing among you except Jesus Christ, and Him crucified" (1 Corinthians 2:1–2). How simple! The very heart of selfless love.

Later, in 1 Corinthians 14, we find Paul not *commissioning* prophetic ministry—Jesus had already done that. He was rather *disciplining* prophetic ministry that was out of order because the people had fallen into a focus, not on the cross, the blood and the selflessness that brings freedom and joy, but rather into an obsession with the gifts of the Spirit. This misfocus led to pride, and pride led to hurtfulness. At root, Paul called for the Father heart of love to be restored to the exercise of the gifts of the Spirit. This can only flow from the depths of the cross, the most selfless act of sacrifice ever made.

Is it not time for us to stop worshiping at the feet of the anointing, the gifts and the manifestations, and excusing the sins of those who engage in private compromise while ministering the power? Should we not live, eat, think and breathe the cross where sin is not only forgiven, but washed clean, broken and done away with? Should we not walk in the resurrection that brings us new life, and should we not correctly understand the fruit of this as radical character change? The heart of my Father has become my highest and most consuming desire. Let that heart permeate the prophetic words that follow.

2

GOD'S HEART REVEALED

I find myself thinking, *Okay. Maybe I almost get it.* Since God spoke to me about having His heart, I have been asking Him to show me more and to build it more deeply into my character. My hunger to be like Him has grown into a consuming passion, because the more I see of the Father the more I realize how far short I fall. It simply will not do to major on revelations of the Father's Word and His future without doing so with His heart and character. When we speak in His name, we represent Him. I want to do this accurately, not only in the word spoken but in the spirit in which I deliver it.

The search for the revelation of His heart begins with Scripture and especially with the accounts of the life of Jesus, His deeds and His words, where every line reveals His true nature. John 14:9 says, "Have I been so long with you, and yet you have not come to know Me, Philip? He who has seen Me has seen the Father; how can you say, 'Show us the Father'?" In every word and every action Jesus perfectly reveals the Father.

This being true, then what Jesus says about Himself speaks volumes concerning the nature and character of the Father's heart. Nowhere is this better stated than in Matthew 11:28–29: "Come to Me, all who are weary and heavy-laden, and I will give you rest. Take My yoke upon you and learn from Me, for I am gentle and humble in heart, and you will find rest for your souls."

If Jesus perfectly reveals the Father, then the Father, God of the universe, exalted King, Almighty, Lord of Hosts who speaks and the universe leaps into being, must be gentle and humble in heart. Next time you sing "Holy!" in a worship service, keep these two words in mind: *gentle* and *humble*. How could God be gentle and humble? God's own heart is gentle and humble.

The Father's Gentle Heart

In the original Greek the word for *gentle* is *praus*. It actually means "gentle and pleasant" and contains overtones of friendliness. It tells us, therefore, that by nature God is easy to get along with. As C. S. Lewis wrote of Aslan, the Christ figure in *The Chronicles of Narnia* (paraphrased), "He may not be tame, but He is safe." He has not burdened us with rules to memorize and regulations to perform. He is simply love. Everything God asks of us, every boundary He sets, serves the purpose of ensuring a love-filled and pleasant life.

I, therefore, stand at odds with the many extreme apocalyptic prophecies of imminent doom, gloom and judgment coming forth right now from so many prophetic voices, and I clearly state that much of what they say is wrong, at least in spirit. Yes, trouble has come to the nation and the world and, yes, it will be around for a long time. Yes, we will see an increase in natural disasters because the earth can no longer bear up under the cumulative sin of mankind. In the realm of economics, things will get worse, notwithstanding limited periods of improvement. The ultimate judgment, however, is yet delayed because God testifies of Himself, of His own heart, that He is gentle and that He is gentle in the extreme.

By biblical standards, ultimate judgment is when your nation stands destroyed, your homes have been razed, enemy troops patrol your streets and your population has been taken into exile. The troubles we now experience are simply reaping for sin sown. Judgment, or more properly wrath (definition to come later), stands yet some distance in the future.

Many so-called prophetic voices that spew condemnation and extreme doom and gloom take their cues from the Old Testament, citing what they believe to be the spirit of the Old Testament prophets. Error! God finally destroyed Israel as a nation-state only after five hundred years of idolatry, infant sacrifice and immorality, and after a long string of prophets had pled with the people to repent. Even then God sent His wrath as a last desperate attempt to purify the people and deliver them from the sin in their hearts and deeds. Ultimately, therefore, God intended even Israel's doom for Israel's good, for cleansing and restoration as opposed to mere punishment. Judgment is not punishment but rather that which separates the precious from the vile, an act of love, a Father disciplining His children for their good.

All through Israel's history our gentle, humble God pled with His people, longed to release blessing on them and protected them even when they deserved punishment. As a last resort, in 722 B.C. for the northern kingdom and in 586 B.C. for the southern kingdom, He finally and reluctantly sent destruction. Then, a thousand years after the establishment of the Davidic kingdom, He sent Jesus to be the perfect sacrifice to deliver us from the sin we could not conquer on our own and to restore us to ourselves. Love is patient. Love is kind. It does not seek its own (see 1 Corinthians 13).

The Father's Humility

Tapeinos means "to be humble, modest or obedient, to stoop, to stoop low or to make oneself low." God humbles Himself and stoops low to lift us. He abases Himself and gets Himself dirty to come to us and carry us to redemption at His own expense. The humble person makes himself or herself small in order to exalt others. At the core of anything truly prophetic stands the heart of the Father and the testimony of Jesus. Quite apart from being a ticket to exaltation, significance or importance, this begins with going lower in order to lift others higher.

John the apostle said it: "In the beginning was the Word, and the Word was with God, and the Word was God" (1:1). "And the Word became flesh, and dwelt among us, and we saw His glory, glory as of the only begotten from the Father, full of grace and truth" (1:14). Jesus went lower to lift us higher.

Here lies the heart of the prophetic. Our humble God makes Himself low, ever ready to abase Himself, to bear the shame for our sake, and all in the name of love that lifts us to a higher place. Would you bear someone else's shame in order to lift him or her higher? Would you call that prophetic ministry? "Beloved, let us love one another, for love is from God; and everyone who loves is born of God and knows God. The one who does not love does not know God, for God is love" (1 John 4:7–8).

The Spirit We Are Of

Luke 9 reports an incident in which Jesus rebuked the disciples for missing the Father's heart.

> When the days were approaching for His ascension, He was determined to go to Jerusalem; and He sent messengers on ahead of Him, and they went and entered a village of the Samaritans to make arrangements for Him. But they did not receive Him,

because He was traveling toward Jerusalem. When His disciples James and John saw this, they said, "Lord, do You want us to command fire to come down from heaven and consume them?"

Luke 9:51–54

In righteous indignation they wanted fiery judgment to fall on those sinners. Worse, they wanted to be the agents of that destruction. "But He turned and rebuked them, and said, 'You do not know what kind of spirit you are of; for the Son of Man did not come to destroy men's lives, but to save them'" (Luke 9:55–56).

This is why prophecies of extreme and imminent doom, gloom and apocalyptic judgment are at best unbalanced. Understand the heart of God. Of what kind of Spirit are we? We must go lower. We must come under in order to lift, not beat the people from on high. Yes, hard times have come and will remain, but as yet we are under judgment only, not wrath.

At some point in the future, wrath must indeed come in the form of destruction of the present evil age in order to make way for the glorious Kingdom of God, but that time is not yet. The Church has yet to learn what kind of Spirit we are of, and if Jesus is to return for a Bride without spot or wrinkle (see Ephesians 5:27), then His coming and the wrath to fall with it must yet be delayed.

While Jesus comes for His Bride, the Father comes for His sons and daughters. When those sons and daughters have been alienated or lost, even by means of their own choices, the true Father humbles Himself to build a bridge to them, not waiting for them to build a bridge to Him. He does so with pleading and with love long before He cuts them off and gives them up. God did this in ancient Israel and He has not changed. While prophets of doom and gloom, therefore, proclaim the extremity of what must ultimately come upon the world, I say that God is not yet finished pleading. The hard times we see today and those yet to come over the next few years will not yet amount to collapse. God's discipline is here, but not yet His wrath. "For those whom the Lord loves He disciplines, and He scourges every son whom He receives. It is for discipline that you endure; God deals with you as with sons; for what son is there whom his father does not discipline?" (Hebrews 12:6–7).

Because our God exists eternally as both a Father and a Son, He sees the relationship from both sides. I am a father to my children and I am a son to my God. I must, therefore, minister with the heart of a father and speak from the position of a submissive son. I, therefore, pray, "Lord, teach me the heart of Jesus the Son and teach me the heart of God the Father." Let every revelation come through their nature, molded by the heart of the Father and delivered through the heart of the Son.

A Prophecy Regarding Prophets

The current prophetic movement is headed for a train wreck. In days to come we will see much of the prophetic world discredited. Many names that have risen to the top of the charismatic A-list will be marginalized, while names that have remained relatively hidden will be revealed and lifted up. The basis for this will be whether or not words presented as prophetic have been fulfilled, but even more, the determining factor will be whether or not prophetic words delivered exhibit the Father's heart and Spirit.

It has been commonly accepted that prophetic anointing does not mix well with pastoral calling. The prophet/pastor has been rare, but this is changing. "Pastoral" as a concept derives from the idea of "shepherding." We serve the Good Shepherd. Psalm 23, the most well-known of all the psalms, begins with, "The Lord is my shepherd." As the world descends into increasing turmoil, the true prophets of God will speak increasingly with the Shepherd's heart that has been ingrained into their own character. Those who will not or cannot walk with a shepherd's heart will find themselves sidelined. Look for major ministries to shrink or fade away while others rise to take their places.

God is love. Therein lies the heart of the Father. Little of the prophetic movement has reflected that heart. Too long have we labored under a defective understanding of the true nature of love. The spirit of religion has blinded us and put a hard edge on our words. In too many cases the word has come through the brokenness and the unhealed heart of the speaker and has failed to communicate the heart of the One who gave it. The coming wave of revival will be an *agape* love revolution. In days to come, God will remedy our deficient understanding of love, and prophetic voices will play a significant role in releasing it.

We must learn the Father's humility and become willing, even hungry, to go lower. We must cease to be those who speak from on high with heavy words of doom and gloom and become those who come under and lift, even when confronting sin and delivering words of warning. The Church and the world must sense the depth of our love and the life-giving nature of the Father's heart. I find this to be all too rare in current prophetic circles. Too many prophetic words these days inspire the wrong kind of fear. Scripture says, "There is no fear in love; but perfect love casts out fear, because fear involves punishment, and the one who fears is not perfected in love" (1 John 4:18).

Prepare, therefore, for a major shift in prophetic ministry that will result in disapproval for some and exaltation for others. A changing of the guard approaches. Our Lord will not long allow Himself to be misrepresented, but will move to vindicate His own name.

39

3

TOWARD A GENUINE REVIVAL

For a number of years now I have been troubled in my spirit concerning revival, the state of current revival centers, past moves of God and trends leading to the future. For a very long time, something has been wrong in the revival stream. Although I have not been able precisely to identify the source of my discomfort, I have, nevertheless, settled on a few things.

Having said as much, know that I am *not* saying that much of what is going on is false, because God is really and truly moving even in the presence of error. I *am* saying that something is wrong and that much is missing.

Four Biblical Elements of True Revival

And suddenly there came from heaven a noise like a violent rushing wind, and it filled the whole house where they were sitting. And there appeared to them tongues as of fire distributing themselves, and they rested on each one of them. And they were all filled with the Holy Spirit and began to speak with other tongues, as the Spirit was giving them utterance.

Acts 2:2–4

Four simple biblical elements must be present in balance for there to be a foundation for real revival.

1. God Comes in Power

First and foremost, God shows up "out of the box" in power to do things we can neither understand nor control. This includes observable physical manifestations of His presence. At such times God often does things for which there is no precedent, like the gift of tongues. For instance, Peter preached that the outpouring on the Day of Pentecost was a fulfillment of Joel 2:28–32, but Joel prophesied only that the Spirit would be poured out in dreams and visions. His prophecy said nothing of the gift of tongues, which has no precedent in any part of the Old Testament. God acted "out of the box."

2. Repentance

When the Spirit fell on the Day of Pentecost and a crowd of thousands gathered, Peter began to preach.

"Therefore let all the house of Israel know for certain that God has made Him both Lord and Christ—this Jesus whom you crucified." Now when they heard this, they were pierced to the heart, and said to Peter and the rest of the apostles, "Brethren, what shall we do?" Peter said to them, "Repent, and each of you be baptized in the name of Jesus Christ for the forgiveness of your sins; and you will receive the gift of the Holy Spirit. For the promise is for you and your children and for all who are far off, as many as the Lord our God will call to Himself."

Acts 2:36–39

The first word out of Peter's mouth when the people asked, "What shall we do?," was the command to repent. The second element essential to genuine revival must therefore be deep and brokenhearted repentance in response to God.

3. Covenant Bonds in Love

And all those who had believed were together and had all things in common; and they began selling their property and possessions and were sharing them with all, as anyone might have need. Day by day continuing with one mind in the temple, and breaking bread from house to house, they were taking their meals together with gladness and sincerity of heart.

Acts 2:44–46

The third element essential to real revival must be that love, fellowship and covenant bonds form. This speaks to the centrality of the local church in the plan of God. Instantly, the focus fell not on the thousands gathered, although they remained faithful to meet as a large group in the Temple, but rather upon walking it out together, house to house in covenant love.

4. Signs and Wonders

"Everyone kept feeling a sense of awe; and many wonders and signs were taking place through the apostles" (Acts 2:43).

The fourth element of true revival is that God announces His presence and expresses His love with wonders and signs. For instance, in the days following the outpouring of the Holy Spirit on the Day of Pentecost, the lame beggar at the gate of the Temple received healing (see Acts 3). As time passed, such a large number of healings manifested that Acts 5:15 says "they even carried the sick out into the streets and laid them on cots and pallets, so that when Peter came by at least his shadow might fall on any one of them."

The by-product or result of all of this comes in Acts 2:47: "And the Lord was adding to their number day by day those who were being saved." The church grew. This is the shape of biblical revival.

Skewed Focus

Today the focus has become skewed and the stream polluted. Much good has been happening, and for this I rejoice, but it has been incomplete and unbalanced. Before I go any further, however, let me be clear once more. I am not saying that anything going on now is false or that God is not in it. I am saying that much remains unbalanced, impure and incomplete and that we have yet to see the *big* one.

I cry out that we must be careful lest we miss the big one when it comes because it may not look much like what we see now. It will not be characterized by mass meetings led by well-known superstars in regional auditoriums, but will rather be centered in local churches led by faithful pastors, many of them unimpressive in the world's terms, whose names we may never recognize.

Gone is the day when one man or woman can fill an auditorium with thousands of believers content to allow the person on the platform do it all for them. As God phases out this kind of ministry, the revival to come will be fueled by the gifts of everyday believers living in covenant with one another so that Jesus, not the mega-ministries, will get the glory. Because of this, the coming outpouring—already unfolding—will reach many more people than any large national or international parachurch ministry ever could.

A greater move of God approaches that will be pure, balanced and complete. In every way it will be the real thing and we will need to be discerning enough to see it and flow with it. First, however, will come a great wave of disillusionment with current practice. It has already begun. People I have known for much of my life as champions of revival are quietly not getting on board with certain developing trends or have been registering their discomfort in their writings. Sensing something not quite right, they have been holding back. We must pray that a growing sense of disillusionment will not turn people off to the real thing when it comes, but that they will come home to the places where the genuine outpouring manifests.

The Issues

Some key issues polluting the stream follow and will be elaborated on in subsequent chapters.

Where Is Repentance?

First, where is repentance and the cross these days? By His stripes we are healed, and at the cross He took our infirmities (see Isaiah 53). We access this mercy through repentance. In Acts 2, Peter presented repentance as the prerequisite for receiving the gift of the Holy Spirit. "Peter said to them, 'Repent, and each of you be baptized in the name of Jesus Christ for the forgiveness of your sins; and you will receive the gift of the Holy Spirit'" (Acts 2:38).

Every revival that ever impacted my nation in a way that transformed our society had at its center the cross, the blood of Jesus and repentance. It seems to me that our emphasis today falls not on repentance and righteousness, but on power, signs and wonders. We seek to be supernatural, while character issues suffer neglect. Every once in a while, almost as an afterthought, we nod politely in the direction of the cross and mutter, "Oh, yeah. It's the cross. We should repent," and then quickly move on to something more appealing than the broken heart and the contrite spirit.

The Biblical Plumb Line

As we focus on power, signs, wonders and healing, where is the biblical plumb line for much of what is said, taught and practiced? The apostle wrote,

> Now these things, brethren, I have figuratively applied to myself and Apollos for your sakes, so that in us you may learn *not to exceed what is written*, so that no one of you will become arrogant in behalf of one against the other.
>
> 1 Corinthians 4:6, emphasis mine

There is no new truth apart from Scripture and no special revelation. No practice in ministry, doctrine of healing, approach to deliverance or any other endeavor stands exempt from testing by a biblical standard. Anointing and the presence of God do not give us permission to move beyond anything written for us in the Word of God.

In spite of this, in revival circles I see us gradually moving toward exalting experience as the measure of truth rather than adhering to the unchanging Word of God. Shipwreck of the faith looms for an unfortunate number of people.

Off-Balance Emphasis

As I have already indicated, I see an off-balance emphasis on power and experience as sources of truth. I have actually heard major leaders state that we live in a post-biblical age when God moves in such a revelatory way that we no longer need to be bound to the Scripture in our teachings, ministries, practices or methods.

It becomes acceptable, therefore, to push people down or knee them in the stomach when they have fourth stage colon cancer as we all saw Todd Bentley do in the Lakeland Revival some years ago—and the man was *not* healed. We fail to question when a healing evangelist, whom I will not name, calls on people to run laps around the sanctuary to contend for their healing. Where did Jesus ever tell anyone to contend for his healing in any manner at all? In the ministry of Jesus, healing was an accomplished gift, not a labor. It was to be received, not claimed. In some circles we continue to tell people to confess that they have been healed when in fact they have not been healed. Where did Jesus ever tell anyone to do anything like that?

We believers have a tendency to accept aberrant ideas and practices when we believe God has spoken to us, when these things seem to work, when they excite our senses and if the anointing seems to continue. We buy in to these things because we feel power in the room, but never seem to question whether Jesus ever did or said them. Experience, rather than the Word of God, has become the measure, the validation, the test of what is true and right.

On this basis it becomes acceptable to speak openly of being caught up to the third heaven as so many prophets do today, and to tell everyone what we saw and experienced there in spite of 2 Corinthians 12:2–4:

> I know a man in Christ who fourteen years ago—whether in the body I do not know, or out of the body I do not know, God knows—such a man was caught up to the third heaven. And I know how such a man—whether in the body or apart from the body I do not know, God knows—was caught up into Paradise and heard inexpressible words, which a man is not permitted to speak.

Caution!

So uncomfortable was Paul with saying anything about that experience that at first he refused to identify himself as the one he spoke of. By contrast, today we blab openly of third heaven experiences on international television. Danger! Our culture teaches us that if we experience something it must be true, but each step we take in the direction of exalting experience above the plumb line of the Word of God moves us farther from the sure foundation and closer to shipwreck.

It seems that if we hear teaching that fails to line up with the Word of God, but is nevertheless delivered in the context of a genuine visitation of the Holy Spirit, then we believe the false teaching must be true because we had an experience. In the real, complete and balanced revival yet to come, however, we must test experience by the Word of God, define experience by Scripture and recognize the true and the right by that test. "Beloved, do not believe every spirit, but test the spirits to see whether they are from God" (1 John 4:1).

"But know this first of all, that no prophecy of Scripture is a matter of one's own interpretation, for no prophecy was ever made by an act of human will, but men moved by the Holy Spirit spoke from God" (2 Peter 1:20–21). We must learn to cease interpreting the Bible in ways not intended or understood by the authors. Peter continued:

> Therefore, beloved, since you look for these things, be diligent to be found by Him in peace, spotless and blameless, and regard the patience of our Lord as salvation; just as also our beloved brother Paul, according to the wisdom given him, wrote to you, as also in all his letters, speaking in them of these things, in which are some things hard to understand, which the untaught and unstable distort, as they do also the rest of the Scriptures, to their own destruction.
>
> 2 Peter 3:14–16

Peter warned against distorting the content of Paul's letters and said that destruction results from this distortion.

These days too many teachers distort the Word in order to justify things that cannot stand the test of Scripture when read

in light of the intended meaning of the authors. Peter continued: "You therefore, beloved, knowing this beforehand, be on
your guard so that you are not carried away by the error of un-
principled men and fall from your own steadfastness" (2 Peter
3:17). The key point: Do not allow yourself to be carried away.
Desperately God wants us to receive revival. He longs for us to
experience His wonders, but we do not have to throw our brains
on the table to do it. Stand this ground and we will "grow in
the grace and knowledge of our Lord and Savior Jesus Christ"
(2 Peter 3:18).

The Corinthian Problem

Arguably the most anointed church in the New Testament,
Corinth had it all. The gifts flowed in power—tongues, healing,
prophecy and more—even as they abused what God was giving
them. On the basis of the gifts of the Holy Spirit that various
ones of them exercised, they began exalting one person above
another. Pride became a problem and hero worship took root
based on the gifts certain ones exercised. They regarded some
as "haves" and others as "have-nots" and had begun to worship
and exalt spiritual superstars in their midst.

They believed, as we tend to today, that the Lord's continuing
presence and the exercise of His power validated their imbalances, but their imbalances and abuses drew stinging rebukes
from the apostle Paul. They thought, *God is showing up so
what we're doing must be right.*

Wrong.

Paul wrote, therefore, in 1 Corinthians 13:1–3,

> If I speak with the tongues of men and of angels, but do not have
> love, I have become a noisy gong or a clanging cymbal. If I have
> the gift of prophecy, and know all mysteries and all knowledge;

and if I have all faith, so as to remove mountains, but do not have love, I am nothing. And if I give all my possessions to feed the poor, and if I surrender my body to be burned, but do not have love, it profits me nothing.

If we read this in its context as Paul meant it to be received, we must regard it as a backhanded slap in the face bordering on insult designed to shock the Corinthians out of their error.

Rewind to Acts 2 and note the love that took root in that first church. The Holy Spirit fell and immediately they began to nurture relationships of love, covenant bonds and the joy of being together. They met in one another's homes and sacrificed for one another. Until that kind of thing happens, we will not see revival, but rather an empty shell making a lot of noise.

By contrast, in Corinth they had the power, the signs and the wonders but little grounding in love or in Scripture. As a consequence, sin and immorality crept in, just as they have today, and for many of the same reasons. Paul found himself forced to rebuke them sternly for tolerating the presence of a man in their midst who was sleeping with his father's wife and had refused to repent. "You have become arrogant and have not mourned instead, so that the one who had done this deed would be removed from your midst" (1 Corinthians 5:2).

In the second half of chapter 6, he chastised them for other forms of sexual immorality and in the first half of that chapter for taking one another to court. They had power without love and they had signs and wonders without a grounding in the Word of God. Unrighteousness and immorality of every kind resulted, just as in our culture today.

Then, as now, such an atmosphere carried little consciousness of the need to repent. Without repentance there can be no character of Jesus imprinted into believers, and without the character of Jesus power may be demonstrated, but that demonstration will fail to carry the revelation of the true nature of the righteous God of heaven whose love passes our under-standing. Our leaders, therefore, fall into sin even in the midst of genuine signs and wonders while our critics have a field day pointing the finger. We have become too much the church in Corinth and not enough the church in Acts. If we will seek holiness, God will give us power and experience, but if we seek power we may miss holiness. Disaster will result.

Are Extended Meetings Really the Way?

This may sound quite strange to many who read it. Rest assured I remain what I call "a revival hound." I do, however, believe we have a misplaced fascination with extended nightly meetings in a region, believing that such meetings will spark or sustain revival in local churches. Again, I believe this to be untrue and unbiblical.

In August 2008, after Todd Bentley's moral compromises had been exposed, the Lakeland Revival left the ten-thousand-seat tent and returned to the seven-hundred-seat sanctuary at Ignited Church. In the second week of August as one pastor who had been deeply involved led the service at his church, he made an appeal. He stated that since the revival had begun, his people had scattered. His next words tore at my heart as he cried out to his own flock to come home. The positive effect of the Lakeland Revival on local churches was negligible and in some cases destructive. Extended meetings in a central location tend to draw people and resources out of local churches when God's plan has always been centered in the local church.

When the Spirit fell on the Day of Pentecost, the Church did not enter into extended meetings in a central location led by a superstar. Rather, meeting from house to house and developing relational love, they began nurturing covenant bonds between people. They did this in addition to worshiping faithfully as a large body in the Jerusalem Temple just as they had always done. As a result, the Church grew exponentially.

If we have all the power but neglect relationships, love and covenant bonds, then we have nothing but noise. God wants a people who, in their covenant bonds, exhibit patience, kindness, humility, selflessness, refusal to be provoked, absolute forgiveness, ability to bear all things, believe all things, hope all things and endure all things for one another (see 1 Corinthians 13).

When that kind of love comes accompanied by the power and presence of God, we call it revival. Until that happens, what we erroneously call revival will never be much more than a man on a platform working his gifts on an audience, or God pouring out an invitation with power upon a deafened people unable to hear.

It cannot be about the man on the stage. It can only be about Jesus. It cannot be about the anointed leader, but rather about *your* gifts, *your* service and the power of the Kingdom of God given to *you*.

Read 1 Corinthians 12 where the apostle taught that to each one is given the manifestation of the Spirit for the common good. God distributes these gifts as tools to deliver the love that takes root in each heart as real revival draws us into the character of Jesus. Until we have absorbed the nature and character of Jesus, until we live as He lived and love as He loves, we cannot call it revival. Until then all we have is the noisy gong or the clanging cymbal.

Past revivals, therefore, filled up and strengthened the churches. Jesus Himself spoke of building His Church. The apostle Paul wrote each of his letters with the intent of strengthening the churches to which they were addressed. The local church has always been the heart of God's plan. Anything that detracts from that focus must be questioned.

Finally

Can we cherish what God is doing, but test men's use of it by the Scriptures once for all delivered? Can we long for and pray for the *big* one, balanced and solidly rooted in God's principles? Can we build a "1 Corinthians 13 church," soaked in love as a vessel prepared to receive the fullness of the presence and power of God? Will each of us ordinary people receive, honor and use our gifts of the Spirit to minister power to this world in the Father's heart?

PART **II**

THE DAYS
TO COME

4

THE DAYS OF AMOS REVISITED

History now rushes forward into the most crucial and strategic period of time in hundreds of years while the Church in the Western world stands largely unprepared and out of position spiritually, theologically and relationally. Sound asleep and riddled with compromise, most of the Church seems functionally blind to the approaching crises, even as warnings appear before us, one after another.

Where we need the selflessness of lives centered in the cross, we have become mired in a culture of self-absorption. Where we need servant hearts and integrity to be modeled in prominent Christian leaders, we continue to see hidden immorality and compromise exposed. Where we need the Church to be the Bride without spot or wrinkle, loving one another with one heart and mind, focused on one goal as the apostle Paul repeatedly exhorted, we have a growing movement drawing believers away from fellowship and covenant connection with a local Body of Christ. Bashing the Lord's Bride has become fashionable, regarded among many even as a holy or prophetic thing. Where we need doctrinal stability to provide a solid foundation for turbulent times, we now have a growing list of bizarre, heretical and unbiblical teachings designed to capitalize on our hunger to be supernatural as opposed to simply living intimately with the Father as His sons and daughters.

We are not ready for the approaching storm, much less the turmoil already unfolding. I believe this to be true in varying degrees across the entire spectrum of movements and groups from revival churches and parachurch organizations to traditional evangelicals. For more than a generation, a culture war of attrition has been raging, focusing us on self and eroding biblical values and morality centered in the selflessness of the cross. Too much ground has been surrendered. This has resulted in serious compromises of essential Christian doctrines, distortions of the meaning of grace, aberrant teachings and ministry practices, abuses of authority, rampant sin—even on the part of respected leaders—and a growing exodus out of the Church. A fire burns in my spirit for a righteous remnant to arise who will stand the ground and become a living vindication of the name of the Lord we serve and love.

Parallels with the Time of the Prophet Amos

Amos prophesied circa 750 B.C. A wealthy sheep rancher and grower of sycamore figs, he lived in Tekoa near Jerusalem toward the end of a period of prosperity just prior to the destruction visited upon God's people by the Assyrians in 722 B.C.

For centuries Israel had existed as two kingdoms, northern and southern, both prospering economically while their immorality and idolatry grew to intolerable levels. Predictably, under the weight of their sin, their society had begun to break down.

A resident of the southern kingdom of Judah, Amos felt a call to speak especially to the northern kingdom, Israel, and to prophesy a warning word of imminent destruction because of their sin. Unable to stop there, however, he also prophesied the destruction of the southern kingdom where the sons of David held the throne in Jerusalem. In both cases he clearly outlined why God's discipline had to fall on them.

Absolutely everything he prophesied came to pass. The Assyrians conquered and destroyed the northern kingdom in 722 B.C. and scattered the population throughout their empire. In 586 B.C., the Babylonian empire destroyed the southern kingdom and Jerusalem with it, then carried the cream of the population into exile for 70 years. God allowed the southern kingdom, Judah, to continue for 136 years after the destruction of the northern kingdom only out of consideration for David, Israel's second and greatest king and the man after God's own heart, because of God's promise that David would never lack a man to sit on the throne.

In Amos 2:4–12, therefore, we find the warnings and indictments he issued. It reads like a carbon copy of developments in America and the Western world today—and for all the same reasons.

Thus says the LORD, "For three transgressions of Judah and for four I will not revoke its punishment, because they rejected the law of the LORD and have not kept His statutes; their lies also have led them astray, those after which their fathers walked. So I will send fire upon Judah and it will consume the citadels of Jerusalem."

Thus says the LORD, "For three transgressions of Israel and for four I will not revoke its punishment, because they sell the righteous for money and the needy for a pair of sandals. These who pant after the very dust of the earth on the head of the helpless also turn aside the way of the humble; and a man and his father resort to the same girl in order to profane My holy name. On garments taken as pledges they stretch out beside every altar, and in the house of their God they drink the wine of those who have been fined.

"Yet it was I who destroyed the Amorite before them, though his height was like the height of cedars and he was strong as the oaks; I even destroyed his fruit above and his root below. It was I who brought you up from the land of Egypt, and I led you in the wilderness forty years that you might take possession of the land of the Amorite. Then I raised up some of your sons to be prophets and some of your young men to be Nazirites. Is this not so, O sons of Israel?" declares the LORD. "But you made the Nazirites drink wine, and you commanded the prophets saying, 'You shall not prophesy!'"

Six Indictments

Here are six indictments from this passage.

1. Rejection of God's Law

Verse 4 says "they rejected the law of the LORD and have not kept His statutes." In the Western world we rationalize away the laws of God regarding basic morality and integrity that He, in His love, revealed in order to secure our well-being. No wonder our leaders fall into immorality and dishonesty!

We divorce at a greater rate than even the people of the world do and then lament the fact that we have so little credibility among outsiders. We make up our own rules and expect God to bless them, then fail to understand why depression, suicide, divorce and poverty are on the rise. Western Christians in their rebellion and self-orientation still engage in ridiculous arguments over whether New Testament believers should tithe. Quote Malachi 3 on a Facebook thread, then witness the lengthy and bitter discussion that erupts. We even question the necessity of being part of a functioning Body of Christ while dedicated Muslims spread Islam like a malignant virus. Radical Islamists line up to martyr themselves while we try to figure out how little we can do and still go to heaven.

Two verses from the book of Proverbs sharpen the issue: "Those who forsake the law praise the wicked, but those who keep the law strive with them" (28:4). For many who claim to be Christian, it has become fashionable to engage in blatant sin and then attack those who speak correctives, accusing them of being religious, judgmental or unloving. Yet Scripture says, "He who turns away his ear from listening to the law, even his prayer is an abomination" (28:9).

2. Belief in Lies

Verse 4 states, "Their lies also have led them astray, those after which their fathers walked." In our culture these lies involve both false gods and demonic philosophies. In a later chapter I will unpack the content and meaning of these but for now a partial list includes: open theism, postmodernism, cheap grace, the idea that once one becomes a Christian there is no longer any need to repent, denial of the existence of hell, universal salvation, bizarre teachings like enhancing your spirituality by taking monoatomic gold pills, consulting Christian astrological charts and much more. A recent teaching beginning to circulate in renewal circles postulates that we have been given the right to command God and that the Holy Spirit will obey our instructions. It is a growing list.

In short, the modern Church increasingly abandons the plumb line of Scripture. In the eyes of the world around us the law of God has become irrelevant, while in the Church it has become a thing to be bent and twisted to fit our own ideas, personal experiences and special revelations.

3. Economic Self-Focus

Amos said, "They sell the righteous for money and the needy for a pair of sandals" (2:6). In the Western world we worship at the altar of prosperity, captivated by a preoccupation with self. The name of this religion is Baalism, Canaan's fertility cult that seduced Israel again and again and infiltrated the worship of the One God. The goal of Baal's sacrifices was economic prosperity. In the Church too many have for too long neglected preaching the selflessness of the cross, the study of which would have pointed us toward character transformation into the selfless image of Jesus. We have instead made prosperity doctrine in all its forms the focus of our faith.

As our culture has increasingly adopted this "religion," we have abandoned our children to rear themselves while we worked two jobs to support flat screen TVs and two-car households—or we brought our recreational drugs into the home and then wondered how we lost our children.

Those of us in the Church bought expensive cars and houses we could not pay for and then protested that we could not afford to tithe. Of course, when the Church then inevitably lacked the resources to care for the poor, we heaped condemnation on it for asking for money and for failing to feed the hungry and clothe the naked.

I often lead ministry teams to Ukraine. In 2009 we arrived in Kiev just as a scandal had broken involving the largest church in the country. The pastor, a foreigner, had been engaged in financial impropriety in the name of the church—some sort of investment scheme related to his prosperity doctrine—and a great many people lost a lot of money. The following year a new government came to power, made up of many who had been Communists under the Soviets. Their conditioned response to abuse was to institute controls. New requirements must now be met when we go to Ukraine on ministry trips and the church in Ukraine labors under a set of restrictive laws regulating the practice of religion. For this we can thank recycled Baalism imported from the West and masquerading as Christian faith.

Amos's indictment of ancient Israel confronted their economic self-focus that led to abuse and exploitation. Although most of us would probably plead innocent to charges of abuse and exploitation, how many of us could do so with real integrity, given the depth of our culturally conditioned focus on self?

4. Sexual Immorality

Verse 7 charges that "a man and his father resort to the same girl in order to profane My holy name." Study of Scripture reveals this verse as just one example of forms of sexual perversion and immorality that had become accepted as normal in Israel. In our culture are we not doing the very same thing? In just a generation we have moved from excessive prudery in refusing to show a married man and woman in the same bed on broadcast television (Ricky and Lucy in *I Love Lucy*, for instance) to openly displaying the entire sex act between unmarried couples. It seems that every show I watch presents jumping into bed out of wedlock as a normal and good thing, accompanied by sweet romantic music.

A leading healing evangelist with worldwide fame falls into adultery, divorces his wife and quickly, sneakily, marries his mistress at the very point of asking for restoration, thus making a mockery of everything a restoration process should mean. A controversy then erupts in the Body of Christ concerning whether or not he should be restored to ministry. There should never even have been a discussion. In other parts of the Body of Christ, leading ministry couples divorce and go right on pursuing their ministries without even a break, as if nothing happened. How far we have fallen!

An overwhelming number of so-called Christians compromise their sexual integrity by watching pornography, or living together before marriage with all the benefits and calling it okay. Universally, they presume upon God's grace to cover their sin, understanding neither the true meaning of grace, which empowers us to live righteously, nor the loving purpose of God's moral law. An increasing number of these actually plead ignorance of that law. How can this be?

5. *Arrogance*

"These who pant after the very dust of the earth on the head of the helpless also turn aside the way of the humble" (verse 7). In reality, neglect of and disobedience to God's laws and principles constitute human arrogance against God, positioning ourselves as though we know more than He does. Our culture actually mocks those who humbly submit to God's law, calling them backward, bigoted, divisive or judgmental. Seldom are they honored who stand for God's moral standard.

6. *Polluted and Compromised Devotion to God*

"But you made the Nazirites drink wine, and you commanded the prophets saying, 'You shall not prophesy!'" (verse 12). Long hair, never cut, marked the Nazirites as those dedicated to the service of God from birth. Among other things, the Nazirite vow forbade the drinking of wine in any quantity for any reason. Not content to keep their sin to themselves, the people of Israel pressured those called to be fully given to the Lord—leaders in the faith—to compromise their commitment. Then, as now, moral failure among the top religious leaders in the nation resulted.

Unwilling to hear the true word of the Lord, Amos's contemporaries sought to silence the prophets who called for complete devotion to God and who pointed out the destruction that would come from unrepented sin. Today, I need only post a statement affirming simple morality on my Facebook page to attract bitter persecution and anger. Anyone standing for righteousness or simple doctrinal truth will be deemed divisive, inflammatory, judgmental or hateful by the culture and even by many Christians who fail to understand the requirements of our faith.

As a pastor, I warn people in love concerning the cost of disobedience in destroyed lives. I refrain from condemnation, pleading only that I would spare them the inevitable pain that I know must result. For instance, in order to save her life, love warns the child playing in the street. In the same way, love confronts those whom God loves concerning the harvest of destruction their sin will bring. I tell them these things on the basis of the Word of God and long observation of real people who suffer real consequences. Nevertheless, many would accuse me of being judgmental and hateful for affirming God's standards and for warning of the destruction to come when sin inevitably fails to deliver on its promises.

In short, in Amos's day the people of Israel wanted to hear what they wanted to hear—not the truth, not the plumb line, not the standard. Today is no different. Hearing would have demanded that the people of Israel change their lives to live not by their own ideas and laws but by the words of God, who set this universe up to begin with and who therefore knows how it works.

At a meeting of prophetic voices I attended in December 2010, someone stated that in our culture we are trying to get to the Tree of Life by eating from the Tree of Knowledge of Good and Evil. Sin cannot produce life.

The New Testament puts this in different terms but makes the same point.

> For the time will come when they will not endure sound doctrine; but wanting to have their ears tickled, they will accumulate for themselves teachers in accordance to their own desires, and will turn away their ears from the truth and will turn aside to myths.
>
> 2 Timothy 4:3–4

In 2:13, Amos expressed God's broken heart over this state of affairs: "Behold, I am weighted down beneath you as a wagon is weighted down when filled with sheaves." God cried, in effect, "I'm fed up! I can't bear it anymore!"

Three Penalties

Hear the prophetic word for the days that lie immediately before us. From these six indictments of Israel, three national consequences resulted. Each of them appears to describe the state of America and the Western world in the present day. Each of them reveals what must transpire in the days to come.

1. Military Defeat

Israel would no longer enjoy the Lord's support to win the battle when the enemy came against them, in spite of being well equipped and strong. "He who grasps the bow will not stand his ground, the swift of foot will not escape, nor will he who rides the horse save his life. Even the bravest among the warriors will flee naked in that day" (Amos 2:15–16). When the invading armies finally attacked, Israel crumbled.

Increasingly, we will see the military might of the United States stymied and limited. Although we won every battle, we lost the war in Vietnam. We should have taken the warning, but in our headlong rush into societal and moral deterioration, we missed it. As I write, we have been mired in extended conflicts in Iraq and Afghanistan, our overwhelming military strength and technology seemingly unable to achieve ultimate victory against poorly armed and outnumbered enemies whose capabilities pale next to the superiority of our armament. As the inevitable consequence of our sin, this kind of frustration will continue and increase in the days to come.

When word of Osama bin Laden's death hit the news, commentators could not stop talking about it. Clips of celebrations in the streets aired on cable television. In no way do I wish to diminish or dishonor the bravery of those who participated in the raid that took him out. I know, however, that bin Laden's death was but one small victory in a wider war, certainly not a turning point. Despite our best efforts, new radicals will arise to take his place and the danger will continue.

Scripture says "not by might nor by power, but by My Spirit" (Zechariah 4:6), but we as a nation have rejected God's Spirit even as we continue to mouth a form of spirituality. American influence in the wider world will steadily decline and we will find ourselves increasingly impotent to significantly affect the course of world events. If elected, a new president may briefly forestall the inevitable, but it will not last. If I have heard correctly, I see a surge of hope in 2013, but it will be temporary because the heart of America and the West will not have changed.

Perhaps more ominous is Psalm 34:7, "The angel of the LORD encamps around those who fear Him, and rescues them." As a nation, America no longer fears the Lord. No longer do we stand on righteous ground. If we did, we would not be seeing one Christian leader after another succumbing to moral failing. If we truly feared the Lord, we would not be struggling with so much corruption both in business and in government. Once upon a time American businessmen were widely admired the world over for their integrity. No longer! If we truly feared the Lord, we would not be seeing Christians casting clearly stated biblical standards aside in favor of their own versions of relative morality.

If real fear of God remained a part of our national character, we would not be forbidden to bring God into public school classrooms. Now, by executive order of the president of the United States, churches cannot even hold a worship service in close proximity (location or time) to a welfare ministry we might provide using government funding. The Faith Based Initiative allows religious groups access to government funding for certain welfare ministries, but those ministries are forbidden to proselytize while delivering those services.

Because we no longer fear the Lord as a nation and have passed this deficit into law, America no longer stands surrounded by His protecting angel. The favor we have enjoyed for so very long has been lifted. Our influence in the world, backed up by military might, will continue to diminish and we will suffer for it. Hatred toward the West—and the United States specifically—will continue to grow and sooner or later a series of significant terrorist attacks will penetrate our best defenses. People will die.

2. Economic Collapse

The unprecedented prosperity that grew as a result of the Lord's favor upon us will be revoked. "I will also smite the winter house together with the summer house" (Amos 3:15). Apparently, judgment on Israel included a collapse of the housing market. Could it really be a mere coincidence that the deepest and longest recession in the Western world since the Great Depression began with a collapse of the housing market?

Economic recovery in the Western world will be limited at best. Do not look for any significant or lasting improvement over the next few years. I do not believe we will see real collapse in the near term but rather extended uncertainty and hardship in which advances that feed our hope of recovery will ultimately be canceled by setbacks. We will see some lift in 2012. Some prophetic voices have already declared the beginning of a season of blessing and prosperity. At first they may appear to be right, but it cannot last. Increasingly, the economic center of the world will shift to China and Asian countries and our own sense of prosperity in the long term will continue to decline. No longer will many of these nations be willing to take their economic cues from the United States.

3. *Closure of Places of Worship*

"I will also punish the altars of Bethel; the horns of the altar will be cut off and they will fall to the ground" (Amos 3:14). God will not permit churches to continue in which His laws, His standards, His morality, His Word and His nature are not honored and taught. Where His Holy Spirit cannot move in freedom He will not permit houses of worship to continue. He is the sovereign Lord.

In recent years a variety of statistics have come out relating to participation in churches in the United States, none of which quotes the same numbers. To validate my point, however, they consistently report that a great many more churches in the U.S. close than are planted each year. The numbers run into the thousands. Millions of believers simply drop out. In the coming years we will see a number of churches, large and small, standing empty, their buildings foreclosed upon, their members having scattered. Already the trend has begun and will accelerate in days to come where the conditions I have outlined prevail and the truth is not fully proclaimed.

Jesus did not call us to inflate our numbers but rather to make disciples. Too many have fallen into seeking numbers of people rather than working to make disciples. Neglect of that mandate will cost the Church dearly in years to come. For example, one very large church in my city substituted another program for its Celebrate Recovery program because Celebrate Recovery mentioned God too much. In yet another large church in my city the young adult pastor has instructed his leadership team not to put too much "God" in their program for fear of alienating unbelievers.

On the other hand, too many others have fallen into the religious spirit and missed the Father's heart. These, too, will lose ground in the days to come.

If all of this reads like gloom and doom, know that this is not the whole picture. For the faithful remnant, the most glorious days we have ever known lie before us. Read on.

5

FIVE YEARS TO PREPARE

I have no wish to prophesy just because I can. Making predictions merely for the sake of making predictions actually seems somewhat self-serving. Being able to say at the end of it all, "See? I was right!," holds no appeal for me. Rather, my heart burns for the Body of Christ, the Church, to see us prepared for what lies ahead. Unfortunately, most of the Body of Christ remain sound asleep at a time when we should be acutely alert and preparing for the most crucial period in history since the first century. We are not ready. I must, therefore, raise the alarm and pray for ears open to hear.

In the mid-eighth century B.C. the prophet Amos said, "Surely the Lord GOD does nothing unless He reveals His secret counsel to His servants the prophets" (Amos 3:7). Certain elements of the Lord's counsel must, therefore, be kept in secrecy, pondered in the heart and held in prayer. I fear many of us in prophetic ministry miss the part where Amos said "secret" and instead speak openly of things that should be held in confidence. True prophets seldom speak all that they know, but rather declare openly only those things God permits them to reveal.

In His love for us, however, God does allow enough to be spoken to enable His people to prepare adequately for the intensity and significance of things soon to come. Often this takes the form of a set of warnings intended to turn us from destructive ways and to articulate the promise of restoration after discipline from the Lord's hand has borne its fruit. Similarly, the Lord's word can alert us to prepare for coming events unrelated to the condition of God's people, much as Agabus prophesied the famine to come so that the Church could prepare effectively (see Acts 11:28).

These days I feel as though much of the prophetic word comes to us as if through a cell phone in an area of the city where the connection tends to fail. We get just half the message before the system drops the call, or before static obscures every third word. Out of our own understanding we then fill in the blanks, getting much of it incomplete or simply wrong. That being said, whether or not I have heard the message 100 percent correctly, we can hardly go wrong by preparing in the ways I call for.

Judgment versus Wrath

The New Testament Greek word for *judgment* is *krisis*. As opposed to punishment or wrath that bring devastation, *krisis* separates the precious from the vile in order to preserve. Judgment—*krisis*—need never become wrath if God's people choose to repent for their sin and turn from evil. For those who submit to it and emerge from it clean and holy, judgment can be a wonderful, freeing thing. For the stubborn heart, on the other hand, it can feel like destruction, but regardless of our response, *krisis* has a redemptive purpose.

America and the Western world currently stand under judg-ment—*krisis*—the separation of the holy and precious from the vile and worthless. Wrath has not yet been released. To avoid wrath, we should welcome judgment. God sends *krisis* as pressure to get our attention and to reveal the failure of our sinful directions, actions and deeds so that we can return to God's ways that produce righteousness, peace and joy.

America and the West yet have time for the kind of repentance and change that turns aside wrath. The current season of *krisis* is God's attempt to separate the precious from the vile at a national and world level, as well as in the Church, in order to avoid being forced to escalate to wrath in order to accomplish the same purpose. Under wrath we pay a greater price. If at all possible God's heart would spare us that. At this writing, we stand perhaps three-quarters of the way through the season of *krisis*. The Church in particular still has time for repentance and change before wrath becomes God's last resort. Unfortunately, for the culture at large, I see no signs of turning. Wrath is certain and the Church must prepare, even if only a remnant hear the call.

Psalm 139:23–24 contains an essential prayer for the days in which we live and we must pray it with all our heart: "Search me, O God, and know my heart; try me and know my anxious thoughts; and see if there be any hurtful way in me, and lead me in the everlasting way." As immorality and compromise run rampant in the Church and leaders fall on a regular basis, this kind of prayer would seem ever more urgent.

Five Years to Prepare

God cannot allow the current state of affairs to continue, either in the Church or in the world. Because He has made righteousness and justice the foundation of His throne (see Psalm

97:2), to allow unrighteousness and injustice to continue would spell the end of His reign. The entire universe would come unraveled. At some point He must act. He is a patient God, however, pleading with His people in love and giving ample time to respond to prophetic warnings.

In July 2009 I had the following dream. I was standing in an open space, perhaps wider than a football field, with the sun at my back and buildings bordering either side. In the distance across that open space, five tornadoes approached, lit by the sun. Unlike tornadoes in the real world, these were neither dark nor black, but more like the white and gray of distant thunderheads on a sunny day. Although these tornadoes came directly toward me between the buildings, I felt no fear, but rather a sense of excited anticipation. A number of people from my church had gathered behind me and I turned to reassure them that this was a good thing and to tell them to prepare for the impact.

Tornadoes symbolize extreme, violent and cataclysmic change. The white coloring suggests that these storms come from the hand of God. The number five indicates that grace would be an essential element in the coming changes. At the time, I applied this dream to my own congregation and then promptly forgot about it until April 2011, when a young adult from my church called to ask me to interpret a dream in which she saw white tornadoes and was not afraid. She thought there were five. I remembered my dream and realized that my interpretation had been much too narrow. This dream applied not only to my congregation but also to the wider Body of Christ.

Now fast-forward from July 2009 to May 2010. That month, as I prepared to make a trip to Toronto for a conference and a series of meetings with pastors from our church network in Ukraine, my brother Mark (spiritual director of Elijah House) sent me a thick file filled with prophecies of extreme apocalyptic doom and gloom. Many of these prophetic words came from prominent names in the prophetic world that many of us would recognize. Mark wanted to know what I thought.

At first, the prophetic prognostications my brother gave me ignited deep fear. Any strong human emotion, whether positive or negative, can distort the prophetic word, serving as a magnifier so that genuine revelations appear larger or more extreme than they truly are. Human emotion can even introduce elements completely foreign to the pure revelation. In order to find the peace of God, the center from which His true voice speaks, I, therefore, had to work at filtering out my anxiety. Similarly, I needed to set aside my own strong desire that these prophesied events not unfold. What sane person would not want everything to be well in this world?

I believe in "zero-based prophecy." In other words, I try to avoid building on the words of others, striving instead to work from intimacy with God apart from the influence of other voices. Building on the words of others leads to distortion and delusion when our human excitement, both positive and negative, comes into play to create the magnification effect. On that basis Jeremiah made a case against the prophets of his day, declaring, "'Therefore behold, I am against the prophets,' declares the LORD, 'who steal My words from each other'" (Jeremiah 23:30). I needed to peel away my personal fears and desires so that I could discern the pure voice of the Lord. Even more, I needed to erase what I had read and begin from nothing.

Airplane flights can be wonderful times to be alone with God, and so as I flew from Denver to Toronto I prayed, worshiped, settled into the Presence and sorted out my feelings. Later, as I soaked in live worship at the conference in Toronto, I began to hear God from a place of rest in His peace. I believe I heard that we have five years to prepare for the more difficult days to come and that while it will be a challenging period of time, it will not be so bad as many have said. Nearly a year had passed before I was prompted to remember the dream with the five tornadoes. Five tornadoes? Five years? Coincidence?

Positive, cataclysmic, even violent change approaches for the Body of Christ. The tornadoes were white, not dark, and five is the number of grace.

Trouble Comes

A time of intensified trouble approaches. It will be serious, more difficult even than the Great Recession under way as I write, and we must prepare to face it. It will not, however, be so horrible as many make it out to be. This is not the end, but merely the days and events leading to and foreshadowing the final events of Matthew 24 and the book of Revelation. I do not know if the number five indicates an indeterminate figurative period of grace in accord with the symbolism of the number five or a literal period of years. If taken literally, then the five years began in mid-2010. In either case we yet have an urgent season of grace in which to prepare. For the Church those God-tornadoes indicate a period of dramatic and ultimately positive change.

The majority of the prophecies in the file my brother handed me were to begin unfolding in the summer of 2010 and intensify into the winter of 2011 and beyond. They included predictions of the catastrophic collapse of the American dollar, runaway inflation, food riots in the streets of America and even the breakup of the United States. I do not believe in "rubber prophecy," stretching what was predicted to make it fit what actually came to pass. Clearly, therefore, at this point those prophecies have been shown to be inaccurate. Nothing that actually unfolded in the fall or winter of 2010 and 2011 can be stretched or made to fit. Nothing happened in fulfillment of those words. Some of us, therefore, need to settle down, stop living in the apocalyptic future and begin to do what we must do now in order to prepare ourselves for what must come. I repeat that it will be serious, but not so bad as many fear.

As American influence declines, crises will accelerate on a world scale. Currently, some world governments and agencies have entered into discussions intended to lead to the end of the reign of the U.S. dollar as the world's reserve currency. Reliable economists predict that when or if this happens, the United States and the world will experience runaway inflation. City, state and federal governments currently face impending bankruptcy. Many other indicators exhibit troubling signs.

In addition to the crises these changes will bring about in the world's balance of economic and military power, we will see ever-increasing natural disasters. The recent earthquakes in Haiti, Peru, New Zealand and Japan are mere harbingers of what will yet come. Volcanoes will erupt in populated areas as stresses on geologic faults increase. Weather disturbances will become more frequent and more violent, leading to flooding and other forms of destruction.

Any follower of current news knows that all of these things are currently unfolding. Expect much more. Earth can no longer bear up under the accumulated sin of mankind and has begun to react in pain as the whole of creation strains to bring forth the new creation in Jesus our Lord. "For we know that the whole creation groans and suffers the pains of childbirth together until now" (Romans 8:22).

This planet is not an inanimate object to be defiled and exploited with impunity. In the book of Genesis, after Cain committed murder, his brother Abel's blood cried out to God *from the ground* (see Genesis 4:10). Multiple Scripture references speak of the trees clapping their hands. Jesus said that if the children were silent the very rocks would cry out (see Luke 19:40). Romans 8 speaks of a creation that longs and travails. More than mere metaphor, these references point to a long, slow consciousness that now reacts to the accumulated defilement we have heaped upon it.

How Then to Prepare?

I have no expertise in economics beyond common sense. Neither am I a meteorologist or geologist. As a pastor, my vision focuses on God's people, the Church. I see, hear and speak from that perspective. Concerning financial protections, investments and related issues I can, therefore, give little advice. Storing up food against potential shortages may be a futile endeavor because as believers we would be called to give it away anyway. I can speak only to spiritual preparations and elements of character the Body of Christ must work to develop.

Refocus Your Comfort Level

The average congregation in America numbers approximately eighty or ninety attendees on any given Sunday morning. Often this results from a subconscious anti-growth mentality rooted in a self-centered concern for personal attention, significance and comfort. Not only is this an insult to the Lord who died to save all men and women, but in the days to come we will need twice the people and resources to meet the same level of need that confronts us today. As governments and agencies fail and become unable to fund various services and programs, refugees from the cultural and economic storm to come will look to the Church for solutions to practical needs. We will, therefore, need twice the number of people contributing their time and resources just to maintain current levels of ministry, and we will need to develop new ministries of love and mercy in order to address new and intensified needs.

We can no longer afford to think in ways limited to our personal comfort and our individual needs. Self-focus is a dead end anyway, failing to deliver on what it promises. We must strive to change our mindset, to cultivate a greater vision more reflective of the sacrificial heart of our Lord and Savior. Spirit-filled churches with the Father's heart must grow significantly. At this writing, extremely few such churches have achieved any significant size. We must choose a passionate commitment to growth of the kind described in Acts where three thousand men and their families came to Jesus in a day "and the Lord was adding to their number day by day those who were being saved" (Acts 2:47).

Fail to do this and we will see many small churches shattered by the hurricane winds of trial that must certainly engulf us in the days to come. Pray for and seek a change of mindset.

Let God Move

God longs to be allowed to be Himself in our midst. On that note, as I have already stated, we will see a continuing and accelerating trend of church closures in places where attitudes, practices and doctrines restrict His freedom. By anyone's measure, thousands more churches close in the United States than are planted in any given year. In many cases this results directly from failure to understand the Father's heart. Too many fellowships treat people with less than honor and freedom, restricting their individual growth in the name of "submission to authority." Where freedom is missing, and where religion—or the dominating and controlling influence of leadership that fails to understand the heart of the Father—takes the place of grace, people leave.

Another cause of decline can be attributed to a growing hunger in our culture for a real experience of God. This culture wants to be moved emotionally. Conditioned by post-modernist philosophy, most people consider experience to be the measure of truth. In this culture, no doctrine, no matter how true, will be accepted apart from the validation experience brings.

Where the Holy Spirit cannot move freely, that experience will not be available. Religion by rote will take its place in some churches, as it already has, while in others it will be "the show," a slick professional performance designed to entertain as much as to communicate the Gospel. Increasingly, as emotional and material needs intensify and fear mounts, people will hunger for more. Nothing less than the unfettered reality of Pentecost, the Kingdom of God and the full force of the truth of God's Word will satisfy that hunger.

The Holy Spirit can be restrained when leadership exercises too much control, when theologies and comfort levels work against His gifts and manifestations and where men run "the show" rather than flowing in His sovereign guidance. A season approaches when people will not come for less than a genuine experience of the powerful touch of God.

Many mega-churches in the Western world have adopted the so-called seeker-sensitive approach, erroneously assuming that the unbelieving and uninitiated cannot deal with extended worship or meaty messages. If that were really true, then why do we see thousands of young people thronging the stages of rock concerts, hands raised, bouncing with the rhythm of the music for hours at a time? Why then can I go to a concert by a well-known folk singer in an auditorium filled with a thousand New Agers and see him hold an audience spellbound for two hours with nothing but his wit, his voice and his guitar? Why? Because there was meat in the music and it was presented with excellence. People *felt* something. They had an experience. Beyond all that, show me any time in history when unbelievers were truly won by a tepid and watered-down Gospel.

We must improve our presentation. We must make room for the Holy Spirit to move. We must communicate real passion and the full truth of the Word. Where God moves, the culture will come, and extended worship, presented in excellence, even when spontaneously created, will carry them into the Presence. Where faithful men and women of God present the meat of the Word, those who have despaired of lives that do not work will listen and come back for more.

The seeker sensitive model will fail as it proves unable to satisfy the intensified hunger that will come with intensified trial. As it does, we will see many churches, once filled with thousands, significantly reduced or standing empty as people leave in search of the real thing. I see this developing already in my own city as some congregations have seen dramatic decline where the Holy Spirit was not allowed to move, or where self-serving versions of the Gospel have been preached. Other churches will be devastated by the exposure of immorality in their leadership, although too much of the Body of Christ really seems not to care. A crisis in the wider Church will parallel the crisis in the culture around us while God redistributes His people and entrusts them to the care of those whose character and integrity reflect His own and whose hearts bear the stamp of His nature.

Cultivate Lighthouse Churches: Four Basic Characteristics

1. Presence-based: Not dependent upon the show, the slick presentation or any particular formula or program, a lighthouse church focuses on seeking and experiencing the presence of God. Worship in a lighthouse church pursues a profound sense of connection with God and will not be halted until that connection is made. Led by worshipers sensitive and responsive to the move of the Holy Spirit, it lasts as long as it takes to open people up to the real presence of God. "Both leadership and laity value the pursuit of the Presence for the honor of the Lord and will not stop until a genuine encounter with God has been achieved."[1]

1. R. Loren Sandford, *The Prophetic Church: Wielding the Power to Change the World* (Grand Rapids, MI: Chosen Books, 2009), 17.

2. God is free to move in any way He chooses: Out-of-the-box things can and do happen as the Holy Spirit inspires them and as His people respond. Historically speaking, unusual, messy, out-of-the-box manifestations and occurrences have punctuated every visitation of the Spirit that has ever impacted any culture. Observers of the outpouring of the Spirit in Acts 2 thought the 120 were drunk. Certainly they did not draw that conclusion by observing them merely speaking in foreign languages. That would have been seen as normal during the Feast of Pentecost when the city was filled with people from many nations. What they saw in the disciples' behavior was consistent with intoxication. From Pentecost onward, revival has always been messy. Wise and sensitive leaders in days to come will make room for this and will shepherd it when it occurs. In days to come, words alone will no longer do.

3. A culture of honor: In lighthouse churches both leadership and laity cultivate a culture of honor, which by definition ascribes worth, value and significance to people, even to the lowest of the low. Lighthouse churches do this for all individuals without exception, no matter who they might be, where they come from or what their condition.

Jesus bestowed high honor on Zaccheus—the betrayer of his own people who collected taxes for the Romans—when He went to his house (see Luke 19). That gift of honor resulted in deep repentance and a changed life. Honor shown to the dishonorable translates into souls saved. It opens the door for the Holy Spirit to convict the hearts of men and women and bring them to repentance and freedom (see John 16:8). The religious spirit can never do that.

From top leadership to the least of us, respect, encouragement and uplifting must prevail. Lighthouse churches work hard at relationships and at ministry structures and strategies that foster love relationships, knowing that relational love stands at the core of the Kingdom of God and flows from the Father's heart.

4. *A healing atmosphere:* Lighthouse churches cultivate a healing atmosphere and diligently pursue specific healing ministries both for the physical body and for life's hurts in order to demonstrate the love of God and His restorative power to a world in need. Once more, the Father's heart and the gift of honor are key.

Reject the Anti-Church Delusion

Currently many have become part of a movement that can only be described as anti-church. Behind it stands a demonic influence that makes this delusion seem both right and holy, as if it were the latest prophetic revelation from the throne of God to declare the demise of the organized church as an evil entity. Excrement!

The enemy of our souls has sought to alienate Christians from church so that there will be no healing beacon for people to identify when the coming crisis engulfs us, and so that welfare resources and other help that churches provide will be diminished. Isolated Christians have few resources with which to minister to the world's needs. This will become even more clear when the scale of the coming crisis becomes evident. Organized churches are the biggest provider of welfare services in the United States, bar none, and always have been. Part of our preparation for what must come involves churches ramping up their welfare programs to feed the hungry and clothe the naked. This takes us back to the need for growth in people and resources.

In the context of teaching concerning our interconnectedness and the ways in which we need one another, 1 Corinthians 12:13 declares, "For by one Spirit we were all baptized into one body, whether Jews or Greeks, whether slaves or free, and we were all made to drink of one Spirit." The Spirit baptizes while the fellowship of the Body of Christ is the medium into which He immerses us. The Bible knows nothing of believers not connected to a local Body of Christ in covenant commitment. Heaven itself is relational, a place of active love.

Lighthouse churches will arise in these last days as islands of glory in a sea of mud, oases of healing in a growing desert of destruction. They will understand the Father's heart and will create a culture of honor and love.

In days to come no longer will many people be won by healings, signs and wonders. These will continue in lighthouse churches as expressions of the Father's love, but they will not be the strongest draw for the hurting masses. Too many famous miracle workers and well-known healers have fallen morally and been publicly exposed. Too many have looked the fool on Christian television. As a result, the world around us is no longer impressed. In this increasingly fatherless culture, the light that draws the hurting multitude will be the Father's love. That love brings the true healing for which the world longs.

Watch, therefore, for an *agape* revival in churches open to receive it—not a revival of cheap grace, but a real revival of true sacrificial and redeeming love from the Father's heart through His people. Manifestations of laughter, falling and shaking will continue as we have seen in the past, but these will be merely the froth at the top of the glass. The true substance of revival will be a surge of deep God-inspired love. In all the four characteristics of lighthouse churches mentioned above, the Father's love will be the thread unifying the whole.

Respond As a Righteous Remnant

For the anxious longing of the creation waits eagerly for the revealing of the sons of God. For the creation was subjected to futility, not willingly, but because of Him who subjected it, in hope that the creation itself also will be set free from its slavery to corruption into the freedom of the glory of the children of God. For we know that the whole creation groans and suffers the pains of childbirth together until now.

Romans 8:19–22

The good news is that during this coming period of intense crisis a remnant will arise who can be called "the sons of God" or "the children of God." *Sons of* and *children of* are adjectival Hebraisms that carry over into the original New Testament Greek. They describe a remnant yet to be revealed who have paid the price to become Christlike in their character—God-like ones, carrying and exhibiting the true heart of God. Creation cries out in anguish for these to come forth. A generation of believers and leaders, filled with a passionate love of God, broken and contrite of heart, refined in the fire, having learned how to love, will emerge in the midst of the crises to come. By their character, integrity, love and Kingdom authority, they will vindicate the name of God and redeem the image of the Church.

In a later chapter I will elaborate further on this, but, for now, know that a great shift, already underway, will come in Christian leadership. As God continues to expose hidden sin in many of the big names we have known, He will reveal His true sons and daughters whose hearts have been cleansed and who will lead the Church as true shepherds. These will stand forth to call us once more to the passionate love of God, our foundation in the cross, the blood of Jesus and the true heart of the Father.

Although the crisis to come may not be as dire as some predict, it will certainly come. We must use the current season of grace to effectively prepare for it. The book of Revelation tells us that a deeper crisis, the apocalypse, will follow after this one before the Lord's return, but that is another season.

Conform to the Image

We must nurture a desperate hunger to become more fully like Jesus, holding nothing back, and we must be willing to pay any price necessary to reach that goal. Each of us must long for Him to remove the impurity from our hearts and lives. Remember *krisis*? Most of us live day-to-day as a mixed bag of good and bad, right and wrong. We deal poorly with adversity and respond to it out of that mixture. As a result, too many believers, steeped in the aberrant, cross-less and self-serving theologies of our day, face the pressures brought on by *krisis* and think that God somehow broke the contract. Their faith shaken, they fall into depression and even anger at God. Under this pressure, many leave the Church in disappointment and frustration. Others simply settle for religion by rote, going through the motions without real passion. Some even deny the Lord. Wrong decisions!

Romans 8:28 and 29 promise,

> And we know that God causes all things to work together for good to those who love God, to those who are called according to His purpose. For those whom He foreknew, He also predestined to become conformed to the image of His Son, so that He would be the firstborn among many brethren.

Too many of us interpret this passage something like this: "If I get fired from my current job, God will use the situation to give me a better one, or if I suffer an injury due to someone else's negligence, God will make sure I am compensated with a lot of money." In other words, we expect that God will use the situation to actually improve or change our circumstances.

Read the context! The apostle did not promise that our circumstances would change. He promised only that those circumstances would work together to produce the good, while the context makes it clear that the good to be produced has to do with character formation. God uses the circumstances of life, whether or not He changes them, to produce character change in us so that we will "become conformed to the image of His Son." We must allow the pressures of life to mold us into the nature and character of Jesus, especially as those pressures increase. The question, therefore, must not be, "Why has God not changed my circumstances?," but rather, "How can I embrace both the good and the bad in a way that shapes my character to conform to His?" Only the settled character of Jesus in us will prepare us to live victoriously in the difficult times to come. I will discuss this in greater depth in a later chapter.

Prosperity teaching has not prepared us for the difficulties to come. What does self-centered accumulation of wealth have to do with the sacrificial life of the cross?

Most people's approach to inner healing has failed to prepare us for this. We have sought personal happiness and relief from pain as opposed to character change for self-sacrifice in the Kingdom of God.

Prophetic ministry has not prepared us for this. We have hungered for personal prophetic words that promise great destiny and blessing. Did we miss the thrust of the prophetic word in Scripture? Jeremiah plucked up what was not God and planted what was. He destroyed that which did not flow from God and built up that which did (see Jeremiah 1:10). Nathan revealed and confronted David's sin and brought him to repentance and redemption. This is character change, not self-serving, self-centered mush.

We will continue to see hidden sin exposed in a distressing number of prominent leaders in the Christian world as God changes the face and the tone of our leadership. Many shepherds will be fired by the Good Shepherd in the days to come and some nationally known ministries will fade to insignificance. Tools have been given for character transformation, but we have largely either misunderstood them, misused them or ignored them.

Now we pay the price. Ministries like Elijah House, Restoring the Foundations, Shiloh Place and others have been blessed by God for cross-centered character change. In the days to come we will pay for our neglect of these ministries as our moral failures and visible lack of integrity continue to erode our credibility in the world.

On the other hand, those who have embraced the cross and paid the price to become sons and daughters of God will emerge and be honored as both the Body of Christ and the world hunger for someone to lead the way in integrity. A changing of the guard is at hand as the "sons of God" emerge and assume leadership. The righteous remnant will experience an outpouring of God's Spirit greater than on the Day of Pentecost. These will rise to the moment and enjoy the most glorious time of their lives ministering the love and the power of God to those made suddenly and desperately hungry by the failure of sin to deliver on its false promises.

Too many of the doctrines and practices of our day have fed the culture of self-focus in the Church, but the "sons of God" will be centered in the kind of selfless love that led Jesus to the cross. Cross-centered selflessness will prepare us to live victoriously, minister the power of the Kingdom of God and bring in a harvest of souls in the days of adversity that must certainly come. Without it, we will be crushed. We must refocus on the cross and divorce ourselves from doctrines and practices that fail to strengthen that foundation. We must resign the culture of self and return to a Gospel centered in the greatest sacrifice of self ever offered for the sake of others. "For I determined to know nothing among you except Jesus Christ, and Him crucified" (1 Corinthians 2:2).

Yet one more key element of preparation remains. More important than any other, it deserves its own chapter and just might be the one to which we have been most blind.

6

PREPARING IN REPENTANCE

The book of Revelation opens with this header: "The Revelation of Jesus Christ, which God gave Him to show to His bond-servants, the things which must soon take place" (1:1). Note the word *soon*. *Soon* roots the Revelation firmly in the history of the first and second centuries, although much of it ultimately applies to the time of the Lord's return.

The seven churches in the Roman province of Asia (modern-day Turkey) were about to face difficult times and were largely unprepared. John wrote, not primarily for the distant future nearly two thousand years later, but to prepare the churches of his own time to face trials about to descend upon them under the domination of the Roman Empire. Although the Lord addressed specific words to each local congregation in chapters 2 and 3, the remainder of the book applied to all of them. I summarize here only the five churches to whom the Lord issued the call to repentance.

Ephesus

The Lord began with a set of affirmations to the church in Ephesus, and then He said this:

"But I have this against you, that you have left your first love. Therefore remember from where you have fallen, and repent and do the deeds you did at first; or else I am coming to you and will remove your lampstand out of its place—unless you repent."

Revelation 2:4–5

Focus on the word *repent*. The Lord did not call them to return to the feelings they had at the beginning. Emotions can be wonderful and I want to feel them, but I know that ultimately my heart follows after my investment. My feelings will lodge in the place of my covenant, faithfully pursued in acts of love.

The Lord's word through John, therefore, exhorted the church to return to the deeds of love they did at the first. Repentance meant reviving their commitment to one another and to others through acts of self-sacrifice for the benefit of others. Jesus' threat to remove their lampstand meant that if they failed to choose repentance, He would remove His presence and destroy them as a church. We must prepare for the trials to come by returning to acts of love, but the key word for the times to come is *repentance*.

Pergamum

To Pergamum John wrote: "So you also have some who in the same way hold the teaching of the Nicolaitans. Therefore repent; or else I am coming to you quickly, and I will make war against them with the sword of My mouth" (2:15–16).

The Nicolaitans stood for cheap grace, God's love and forgiveness perceived as permission to sin. The Lord, therefore, called once more for repentance, turning away from disregard of God's laws and from a perverted understanding of the meaning of the cross. He called them to stop tolerating those who held the teaching of cheap grace and summoned them to a renewed respect for God's laws and God's will.

A compromising people would be a weak people who could not stand in the trials that must soon take place. The teaching of the Nicolaitans has taken deep root in the Western church. Crisis looms as the return of the Lord draws near and we are not ready. We desperately need a movement of brokenhearted repentance to root out our moral weakness and instill the character of Jesus.

Thyatira

Like her sister churches, Thyatira needed to repent for tolerating compromise:

> "But I have this against you, that you tolerate the woman Jezebel, who calls herself a prophetess, and she teaches and leads My bond-servants astray so that they commit acts of immorality and eat things sacrificed to idols. I gave her time to repent, and she does not want to repent of her immorality. Behold, I will throw her on a bed of sickness, and those who commit adultery with her into great tribulation, unless they repent of her deeds."
>
> Revelation 2:20–22

Under the guise of being a prophetic woman who heard from God, Jezebel taught people to compromise with the idols of the world. In order to operate a business in Thyatira one had to belong to a trade guild. Dedicated to patron gods, the trade guilds held feasts in the temples dedicated to those gods at which the menu included meat that had been sacrificed to idols. Many of these feasts ended in orgies. Here lay the heart of the compromise Jezebel justified under the guise of her supposed spirituality, as she led her disciples into pagan worship and sexual immorality for the sake of what might be called ancient networking. Because it violates our marriage to Him, God calls such compromise "adultery."

Again, therefore, God summoned them to repentance, a turning. Jezebel and her followers would not be ready for "the things which must soon take place" and they were about to suffer the Lord's disciplining hand in sickness and trouble that comes as the direct result of that kind of compromise. A great many of those who call themselves Christian today consistently make the same sorts of compromises. These will be woefully unprepared for what must transpire in the years ahead.

Sardis

Sardis had fallen asleep and lost its passion: "So remember what you have received and heard; and keep it, and repent. Therefore if you do not wake up, I will come like a thief, and you will not know at what hour I will come to you" (3:3).

Yet again God called for repentance as He sought to prepare and strengthen His people for "the things which must soon take place." A church asleep and passionless cannot survive either as a church or as individuals when the trials come. Passionless individuals in our own time will find their hope and their strength robbed in the face of difficulty.

Laodicea

Neither deeply devoted nor quite fallen away, Laodicea had become lukewarm. In modern terms I often encounter the attitude that Jesus is a part of my life but passion is not necessary. Jesus responded to their lack of passion by saying that if they remained lukewarm, He would spit them out and end their life as a church.

The remedy remains consistent. "Those whom I love, I reprove and discipline; therefore be zealous and repent" (3:19). Make the 180-degree turn that constitutes repentance and choose to burn with passion and zeal.

90

A lukewarm church filled with lukewarm people will not be ready or able to stand in a time of pressure. Such a church will never be capable of ministering in the kind of power that makes God's people a force to be reckoned with. In the intensifying trials to come, those who have chosen passion—not those who are waiting to feel it, but those who have chosen it—will heal the sick, raise the dead and change lives. We will see the shrinkage or closure of a great many churches lacking passion over the coming years.

Dedicated Hearts

Bear with me as I reemphasize that we have been granted a period of time, a symbolic or literal five years, to prepare. According to what the Lord showed John in the book of Revelation, the heart of our preparation has little to do with studying how to do signs and wonders or classes in how to pray for healing. It begins with repentance and restoration.

Those things—signs, wonders and healings—result naturally from hearts and lives dedicated and sold out to God. As we take in the message of repentance and choose passion, holiness and character change, signs, wonders and healings will follow and increase. This calls for deep, abiding, heart-rending, God-take-it-all repentance.

I can hear some believers thinking, *What do I have to repent of? I'm a good person. I don't beat my spouse, get drunk, do drugs or lie. I give generously to my church. What's the problem?*

Is your every thought godly? Does every feeling you carry in your heart reflect Him and His nature? Do you never hurt anyone? Is every word that comes from your mouth the right thing? Are all your relationships whole and strong?

Every one of us carries hurts and wounds that we tend to regard as somehow morally neutral. Having been in full-time ministry since 1976, I know that hurts and wounds eventually become infected as our sin nature causes sickness. I have come to regard my own ongoing wounds as sin, even when inflicted by others, because they fail to reflect the heart and character of God.

Just like all of you, I have a closet filled with hurts and wounds built up over the years as others have dealt with me in hurtful ways. I seek repentance because those hurts will inevitably affect the lives of others whether I want them to or not. I wonder if some of us would heal up more quickly if we stopped thinking of our wounds as something to be healed and started thinking of them as sin to be cleansed? As we allow God to remove sin we will find our hearts ever more sold out to the Living God, and that results in strength.

We have been granted time to prepare for the times ahead. We must use it wisely because we are not ready as the Church or as individuals for what must take place. If John were alive today he would be writing the same things to us that he wrote to those seven churches, and he would be calling for the same kind of repentance.

Unfortunately, in our day only a remnant will respond to the call for repentance. The Baal spirit that focuses us on self has effectively anesthetized the culture to any real concern for the impact of sin on others. Consequently, we will not see a culture-sweeping revival in America and the West. We have entered the time of Revelation 16:9 and other verses where the apostle repeatedly lamented that men and women "did not repent" as the judgments of God fell upon the world.

Strengthening

Jesus never wants to come in judgment. Rather, He loves us and knows that intensified pressure from the world is coming. In the

Western world it will not include physical torture, martyrdom or imprisonment as it did in John's day and for many believers in other parts of the world today. For us it will take the form of increasing marginalization as the mainstream of the surrounding culture moves in directions we cannot follow. It will include discrimination against genuine Christians in nearly every aspect of life. For example, many of us will be denied employment or advancement when our superiors find out what we believe in. Jobs will be lost. From the culture around us, condemnation will increase because we will be seen as hateful and dangerous due to our faith commitments with regard to moral issues.

Our Lord knows what weakens us and does not want us to collapse under the pressure. He understands better than any of us what kind of strength it will take to live victoriously in the times to come. As we move into the last days before the Lord's return, trials—birth pains that accompany the coming of the Kingdom of God (see Matthew 24:8; Romans 8:22)—will come with increasing intensity. Already disasters of record proportions abound in the form of deadly storms and floods, earthquakes and tsunamis. Famines persist. Wars multiply.

These will be difficult days for the world around us, to say the least. We will see economic upheaval on a global scale, probably before the middle of this second decade of the current century. Political changes will shake the world. Changes in religious attitudes and the demographics of faith will threaten the foundations of societies. Along with the rest of the world, Christians will be affected by all of these things.

For us, however, the Lord has ordained these coming days as the most glorious of our lives, even if we suffer martyrdom, even if we die, even if the world hates us, even if economic hardship falls upon us. In the midst of this, just as in the days of the Roman Empire, God will ramp up His power. Miracles will increase because the Kingdom of God invades this earth and we get to be part of it. People will suffer and we have been granted the power to alleviate their pain, heal their bodies and restore broken lives.

God calls us to be ready. God is making us ready. Repentance is key. What in me is compromise? Does my living situation reflect His will and law? What in me is broken? Is the relationship between my children and me reflective of the relationship Father God has with Jesus the Son? Do I have the same love for my wife that Jesus has for His Bride, the Church? Do I love His Bride with the same intensity He does? What in me fails to function in the character of the Holy Spirit? Am I at peace as He is? Do I forgive as He does? Is all that is "me" the kind of love that defines His nature? Am I pure in heart as He is pure in heart? Has perfect love cast out my fear to make me fearless and perfectly secure?

If I must answer in the negative to any of those questions, then I have sin in me to deal with and I have brokenness in me that calls for repentance and cleansing. My flesh wants to say that I have come far enough. I am all right now. I took the classes and studied the material. I attended the conferences. The notebooks fill my bookshelf. But am I all right? No. You and I have been forgiven by the cross. We have been made holy by what Jesus did there. God sees us wearing the righteousness of Jesus, not our sin, but that does not automatically right all of our wrongs or change our character. There remains room for repentance, change and growth.

Real Repentance

Two Bible stories in particular illustrate the true nature of repentance. In 1 Samuel 13, King Saul faced an overwhelming army of Philistines. Promising to return in seven days, the prophet Samuel commanded him to wait. Samuel delayed and, as fear mounted and his troops began to scatter, Saul "forced" himself and offered up a sacrifice on his own. Just then Samuel appeared and confronted Saul with his presumption in offering the sacrifice and with his failure to wait as commanded. Saul could only offer excuses and justifications for his disobedience. In the face of this failure to own his sin, God removed the anointing from Saul and, ultimately, the kingship.

David committed sins much more heinous than Saul's, first committing adultery with and impregnating Uriah's wife, then ordering Uriah's death in battle to cover his tracks. When Nathan confronted him with what he had done, David's response differed profoundly from Saul's. He could have attempted to excuse his adultery by pointing out the temptation involved when a naked woman takes a bath on the roof of her home in full view of the man next door. Instead, "David said to Nathan, 'I have sinned against the LORD.' And Nathan said to David, 'The LORD also has taken away your sin; you shall not die'" (2 Samuel 12:13).

David felt the harm he had done to the Lord's heart. In the verses preceding 12:13 he connected with what he had done to Uriah, Bathsheba's husband, in taking what belonged to him and in later having him killed. Unlike Saul, David, known forever as the man after God's own heart, continued as king and ultimately became the ancestral father of Jesus.

True repentance, therefore, puts you in touch with the damage your brokenness or your sin has done to God and others. True repentance takes root when the harm to the heart of God and others becomes more important than your own remorse or pain. Repentance must be focused on God's heart, your child's heart, your spouse's heart or your friends' hearts. Repentance takes root when you feel inside yourself the damage done to others through your sin or your brokenness. Until that happens you can be sorry only for the hurt you caused yourself, and that will never be enough to bring about character change. Without character change, none of us will be prepared to face the trials that must certainly come.

This culture has gone too far. As John foresaw, men and women will not repent, despite the pressure of judgment falling all around them. This will be true because the culture of self has erased a true sense of and care for the impact of our lives and actions on others.

Too often over my many years as a pastor I have heard believers protesting that their sin is private and, therefore, hurts no one else, but there are no private sins that hurt no one else. Every sin weakens the whole Body of Christ. In the days to come we will not be able to afford such weakness. We will need to stand together, not only in simple unity, but in righteousness as well, or be weakened at a time when our full strength will be required.

Damage through Connection

First Corinthians 12:26 says, "And if one member suffers, all the members suffer with it; if one member is honored, all the members rejoice with it." Joshua 7 records a poignant example of the actions of one man affecting the whole people of God. The Israelites had just destroyed Jericho, the first city in the Promised Land to be taken. God had commanded them to sacrifice absolutely all the spoils to Him and keep nothing for themselves, but Achan held some back and hid it in his tent. As a result, the whole nation suffered weakness and defeat at Ai.

When they eliminated Achan and his sin from their midst they recovered and went on to victory. The private sins you and I commit do affect others. Real repentance comes when we get in touch with that, and our effect on others comes to matter to us more than our own welfare.

The enemy of our soul has worked very hard to eliminate consciousness of sin and guilt from modern culture and from the Church. He has convinced too many of us that we are good people whose goodness would be revealed if only we could change our circumstances or receive healing for the wounds we have suffered. As opposed to taking responsibility for our sin, he has convinced us that we are victims of circumstance or of the deeds of others. We tend, therefore, to seek healing instead of repentance. This keeps us weak and unprepared for the days to come, both as individuals and as a people.

The moment you move into real repentance you cease to be a victim and begin to move in the authority of victory. Saul thought he was a victim of circumstance. *I had to do it! The people were scattering from me!* David took responsibility, "I have sinned against the LORD," no longer a victim. Unlike Saul who got himself fired, David remained king in authority. God will pour out His authority through believers in greater measure in these coming days.

Misfocused Pursuits

The modern Church, especially in renewal or River circles, has fixed its attentions on the pursuit of power and blessing. Good things! But power and blessing can never be obtained by taking a shortcut past repentance. True power, real open doors and genuine victories flow through clean vessels. Repentance gets us there.

The church in Philadelphia in Revelation 3:7–13 stood innocent before God. A small church with a poverty-stricken membership, they nevertheless carried the authority of the Lord. They had persevered under pressure, and as a result God opened up opportunities for them to convert even their enemies who would experience the love and power poured out through them. Repentance cleanses. It changes character. Where God sees Himself reflected in our character He grants greater power and authority.

Lack of repentance lost Saul the kingdom. Real repentance got David the power of God to lead the kingdom, to found a dynasty and ultimately to become the ancestral father of Jesus. Why? Because repentance leads to character change and God entrusts power and authority to those who will use and steward it as He Himself would.

A Time Like No Other

Whether or not the world around us repents—and, save for a remnant, it will not—those of us who do hear and humble ourselves in repentance and submission to God will enter into a time like no other from Bible times until now. It will be a time of unprecedented glory in which we will have more fun and walk in more victory than we have ever imagined.

Signs and wonders will multiply. There will be a harvest of souls such as we have never seen and a sense of the presence of God more powerful than any we have experienced. Individual believers will minister in greater power and authority than they have ever known. Even in the midst of world crises, it will be the end of depression and despair for the sons and daughters of God.

A line in the sand is now being drawn in the Christian world, the Body of Christ. The divide deepens between those who fool themselves into believing themselves Christian because they give mental assent to who Jesus is but who refuse to live the life, and those who choose to know nothing but Jesus Christ and Him crucified. These latter choose to give it all to Jesus without reservation and to obey Him at any cost.

The time of the manifestation of Matthew 7:21–23 approaches:

> "Not everyone who says to Me, 'Lord, Lord,' will enter the kingdom of heaven, but he who does the will of My Father who is in heaven will enter. Many will say to Me on that day, 'Lord,

Lord, did we not prophesy in Your name, and in Your name cast out demons, and in Your name perform many miracles?' And then I will declare to them, 'I never knew you; depart from Me, you who practice lawlessness.'"

It is a dividing line between those who want to walk in cheap grace as permission to live in compromise, doing as little as they think they can and still get into heaven, and those who cry out in song and in prayer for God to let them go farther for Him and become more completely abandoned to His love, as Misty Edwards at the International House of Prayer so movingly sings in "Always on His Mind." In other words, we want to go as far as God will allow us to go for Him without reservation.

Acceleration

"Time's up!" How many times have I heard this prophetic pronouncement from the Lord, almost audibly, over the last several years? The time has ended for slumber and playing games. We believers must wake up and come alive. A time of acceleration has come upon us consonant with the beginning of the events leading to the Lord's return. Both good and evil will manifest fruit from their respective roots much more quickly both now and in the years that lie before us.

We will see, and have already seen, an acceleration of events in the world at large. As far back as the 1980s we began to see an increase in the exposure of sin in national leaders, both secular and Christian. We will see acceleration in the manifestation of good fruit, as well. We no longer have either room or grace for lukewarm devotion. John said it in Revelation 3:16 when the Lord rebuked a church living in a situation similar to that which we now face. Persecution was imminent, but as their material prosperity lulled them to sleep the church in Laodicea had grown lukewarm. Passion had faded. "So because you are lukewarm, and neither hot nor cold, I will spit you out of My mouth."

Accordingly, very soon now the Body of Christ in the Western world will become either a strategic people or a forgotten people. A great sorting out of wheat from chaff has been under way. This will continue and intensify in days to come. Very soon now we will see some mega-churches and other smaller ones closing and on the verge of closing. There will be a great redeployment of the people of God to local expressions of the Body of Christ where the cross has remained central and the Holy Spirit has been allowed to be Himself. These islands of glory will be characterized by a passionate, sold-out love of God and by the Father's heart infusing all they do. I choose to be strategic, not forgotten.

On an individual level, for instance, I have seen marriages in which the partners have tolerated certain character flaws in themselves that have affected their relationship for many years. They swept these problems aside and continued to appear solid and secure. Suddenly, in this time of acceleration, trouble has erupted as those old seeds have borne fruit. It used to be said that the honeymoon would last five years before reality and disillusionment set in. The pastoral staff at my church have found that the honeymoon now often ends mere moments into the marriage. God Himself has set in motion an acceleration of exposure in order to force us to deal with brokenness that would harm us in the days to come.

On a positive note, many things we have labored over for many years and seen little fruit will now suddenly begin to break through. Answers to prayer will come more quickly. Those who come to the Lord for the first time will mature much faster than did many of us who came to the Lord decades ago. "Let our sons in their youth be as grown-up plants, and our daughters as corner pillars fashioned as for a palace" (Psalm 144:12).

These are just a few examples of what must happen in this season of acceleration. Put your track shoes on because we will have to run to keep up with what God does in the days to come. In our personal lives, relationships and churches we must stop putting off dealing with areas of our hearts that we have kept hidden or that have yet to be conformed to the image of Jesus. As the time of acceleration intensifies, these things will ambush us to cause disruption and destruction.

We have five years, literally or symbolically speaking, in which to prepare, five years to get ready for a deepening crisis coming upon the world in every area of life—economic, societal, environmental and spiritual. The Church must take hold of repentance and grow in grace, love, devotion, faithfulness and numbers in order to have the people and the spiritual and physical resources available to meet growing needs and to walk in the level of power the times will call for.

7

THE REVEALING OF THE SONS OF GOD

For the anxious longing of the creation waits eagerly for the revealing of the sons of God. For the creation was subjected to futility, not willingly, but because of Him who subjected it, in hope that the creation itself also will be set free from its slavery to corruption into the freedom of the glory of the children of God. For we know that the whole creation groans and suffers the pains of childbirth together until now. And not only this, but also we ourselves, having the first fruits of the Spirit, even we ourselves groan within ourselves, waiting eagerly for our adoption as sons, the redemption of our body.

Romans 8:19–23

And we know that God causes all things to work together for good to those who love God, to those who are called according to His purpose. For those whom He foreknew, He also predestined to become conformed to the image of His Son, so that He would be the firstborn among many brethren; and these whom

He predestined, He also called; and these whom He called, He also justified; and these whom He justified, He also glorified.

Romans 8:28–30

As the title of this chapter and these Scripture quotes indicate, the next prophetic word focuses on "the revealing of the sons of God." Connect this content with what I have already said on that subject and with my previous comments on lighthouse churches and ministries springing up in the years to come and consider it a further unpacking of what has already been stated. In the season before us, you will find "the sons of God" firmly rooted in lighthouse churches and ministries, not walking alone. As ever, I remain the pastor/teacher, so bear with me while I lay the groundwork for what I believe must soon take place.

Revival History

History can inspire us, but it can also tell us where not to go. For the sake of heading off any possible misunderstanding, therefore, I must make it crystal clear what I do *not* mean when I speak of the "revealing of the sons of God."

In the 1940s a movement sprang up under the leadership of William Branham that came to be known as "The Latter Rain." A centerpiece of his teaching came from a misapplication of Romans 8:19 and "the revealing of the sons of God." Drawing on this passage, the adherents of The Latter Rain fancied themselves "the manifest sons of God," a new breed of Christians who would wield supernatural power in the last days and be instrumental in subduing the earth.

They believed that the emergence of "the manifest sons of God" would be the fulfillment of the prophecy of Joel's army spoken of in the prophetic book of Joel. Charismatics and

103

Pentecostals, however, have often been justly accused of doing horrible exegesis. The people of The Latter Rain movement, and many today who believe themselves to be part of Joel's army, seem to miss the fact that Joel prophesied, not an army of believers going forth to conquer evil and win souls, but an army of enemies executing judgment and destruction upon Israel. Depending on your view of the date of Joel's prophecy, he foresaw either the army of the Assyrians who destroyed the northern kingdom of Israel in 722 B.C. or the army of the Babylonians visiting similar devastation on the southern kingdom in 586 B.C. Consequently, while I believe an end time remnant of aggressively passionate followers of Jesus will emerge, it cannot be called Joel's army.

By "subduing the earth" they meant that a militant and aggressive church (Joel's army) would arise to rule the world both politically and spiritually. Today this doctrine undergirds much of Dominionism, the false teaching that we believers will take over the governments of the world, the seven mountains of influence (everything from government to education, from business to entertainment), establish the Kingdom of God on earth and then deliver it up to Jesus upon His return. Scripture, however, clearly teaches that mankind as a whole will not repent and that the Kingdom will only be established on earth by the cataclysmic intervention of Jesus at His return. See Matthew 24 and the book of Revelation to name just two passages of Scripture.

Branham's teaching held that these "manifest sons of God" would be perfected and transformed into their glorified bodies prior to Christ's return, which directly contradicts Paul's teaching in 1 Corinthians 15. This perfection would allow them to subdue the earth for Jesus. In fact, the adherents of The Latter Rain taught that Christians, having a "divine nature," become "gods."

In the end, Branham denied the central doctrine of the Trinity and believed himself to be Elijah the prophet heralding the last days, as well as the angelic messenger to the Laodicean church in Revelation. He taught that anyone belonging to any denomination had taken "the mark of the beast" and would certainly be damned.

Do not, therefore, confuse what I write here with "the manifest sons of God" teaching that came through William Branham and The Latter Rain movement. For many charismatic leaders and prophetic voices today, William Branham remains a spiritual hero. I regard him as a dangerously deluded heretic.

The Truth of Romans 8

The whole of Romans 8 speaks to the redemption of all that fell when Adam sinned. In the beginning God spoke a sinless creation into being that reflected His own perfection, but it became corrupt through Adam's disobedience. The whole earth, therefore, aches and groans for the redemption of mankind because when God redeems mankind, creation itself will be freed from bondage. Our completed salvation will be earth's redemption.

As I noted in an earlier chapter, "sons of God" is a Hebraism—a Hebrew manner of speaking—that carried over into the Greek as a way of describing the nature of a person. For instance, people called James and John "the sons of thunder," meaning that they were probably loud and strong men. Likewise, "sons of perdition" describes those whose lives are characterized by sin and the destruction that comes from it.

"Sons of God" likewise defines those who in some significant ways have come to reflect the nature and character of God. This explains why so much of Romans 8 addresses character change.

So then, brethren, we are under obligation, not to the flesh, to live according to the flesh—for if you are living according to the flesh, you must die; but if by the Spirit you are putting to death

the deeds of the body, you will live. For all who are being led by
the Spirit of God, these are sons of God.

Romans 8:12–14

Changes manifest in our character when the Holy Spirit working in us transforms our nature. It was this kind of "sons of
God" that the apostle meant when he wrote, "For the anxious
longing of the creation waits eagerly for the revealing of the
sons of God" (Romans 8:19).

How we love to camp on Romans 8:28! "And we know that
God causes all things to work together for good to those who
love God, to those who are called according to His purpose."
Also previously noted, in the context of the whole chapter, Paul
intended us to understand that God uses everything that happens to us or around us, good as well as bad, to form His nature
and character in us. Verse 29, therefore, states: "For those whom
He foreknew, He also predestined to *become conformed to the
image of His Son*, so that He would be the firstborn among many
brethren" (emphasis mine). Jesus' life, formed in us, constitutes
the heart of what it means to be seen as sons and daughters of
God. For this purpose we have been called. This is what we live
for and long to become.

Romans 8:28, therefore, teaches us that God uses all of life's
circumstances and events to mold us into the likeness of His Son.
In a similar vein Paul wrote in Ephesians 4:15, "But speaking
the truth in love, we are to grow up in all aspects into Him who
is the head, even Christ."

Living It

In the early 1990s I moved to Denver, Colorado, expecting to
step at last into the place of my anointing. To my great grief, I
fell instead into a long and horrible nightmare. Never before had
I encountered such slander and ugliness directed at me. Never

before or since have I been so beaten down and wounded as in those first years in the Mile High City. How I would choose to respond to and deal with that ugliness in the following days and years would have everything to do with the outcome in my character and with my future as a man of God.

How would I let that trauma change me? Would I learn humility? Would forgiveness become such a foundational element of my nature that in the face of wounding or offense it would never be a question? How would forgiveness as a character trait be built into me at such deep levels if I were not confronted with wounds and offenses against which to exercise forgiveness? The attacks I suffered taught me to return blessing for insult until that became a deeply ingrained part of my character. I could have chosen to respond in some other way, but it would have poisoned my spirit for years to come. Strength grows only when we must exercise ourselves against an opposing force. Because hatred against Christians will accelerate in the Western world in the days to come, forgiveness and the gentle answer that turns away wrath must become second nature to us (see Proverbs 15:1).

In 1990 I suffered through an audit by the United States Internal Revenue Service (our national taxing agency). Because my tax accountant had been incompetent, the audit became a disaster that threatened to drive my family and me into bankruptcy. I felt abandoned by God and betrayed. Because too many other areas of my life were coming unraveled at the same time, I found myself teetering on the brink of a nervous breakdown.

In the midst of this came a moment when I discovered that the auditor had overlooked something that would have saved me $2,500. This would have gone a long way toward getting me through the audit in a way that would avoid financial collapse. I had only to keep quiet and say nothing. I told myself it was not my fault and that I could not be held accountable for the auditor's mistake.

For several days I prayed and struggled with God until in the end I pointed out the error. The look of amazement on the auditor's face is something I will never forget. God uses all things to bring about character change, the good that shines with His nature. I came away from that decision having established something in my character that can never again be challenged. Should a similar situation confront me in the future, there will never be a question. Had there been no test, no force against which to exercise myself, that depth of integrity would never have been strengthened in the way it was.

In years to come, as the world system continues to be troubled, many of us will find ourselves financially stressed. Will you respond in faith, trusting God? Will you allow future difficulties to train and change you for the good, or will you react in bitterness, blaming God and falling into depression? How would faith grow if there were no trials to test you and force the exercise of your character? Or will you compromise your integrity in ways large and/or small in order to get by or gain an advantage, thinking that no one sees?

Perhaps God allowed this test to refine your sense of what you really need and to help you learn to live humbly and at peace with Him. Could it be that your situation exposes unrighteousness in the way you deal with finances so that you develop a deeper sense of integrity? Or will you become bitter and afraid and begin blaming God as if He had betrayed you? Will you submit to God in the time of trial and let Him use it to shape the person you are becoming? All things work together to form you into the image of Jesus, wherein lies our peace and joy, no matter what happens in the world around us.

Our Hope

We must grow up into the fullness of Christ until He can reveal us to the world in all His glory as those who look, sound, feel, think and act like Him. This, our destiny, is also our hope, our reason for being alive and on this earth. Regardless of my situation, I have been destined to become like Jesus. Nothing else matters. Here lies the power of the cross and the resurrection, the working of His Spirit in us.

God wants to reveal us to the world, to show us off as His handiwork as He unveils a righteous generation, carefully formed, in the midst of a world that looks more and more like Sodom and Gomorrah. Many of us have therefore been on a journey. We have lived in the previous chapter, Romans 7, where the apostle spoke of his brokenness and of the exposure of his sin. No tumor can be removed until the doctor sees it on the CAT scan. God, therefore, uses life situations to expose the places where we need surgery. Romans 7 is the CAT scan of Paul's character apart from Jesus.

> For I know that nothing good dwells in me, that is, in my flesh; for the willing is present in me, but the doing of the good is not. For the good that I want, I do not do, but I practice the very evil that I do not want. But if I am doing the very thing I do not want, I am no longer the one doing it, but sin which dwells in me. I find then the principle that evil is present in me, the one who wants to do good.
>
> Romans 7:18–21

In Romans 8 he found the remedy. Therein lies our salvation, our transformation into the image of Jesus. Many of you now reading this book have undergone a CAT scan sent by God to reveal weak and diseased places in the heart so that you can be healed, strengthened and transformed. He has used, and will use, the stresses of life to accomplish this.

For some, the pressure has been the strain of facing a crisis with your children and discovering that you have not been so patient as you have deceived yourself into believing. You really cannot know who you are or where your weakness lies until tested by adversity.

Others have faced difficulties in their marriages. No one reveals your sin like your mate. You have, therefore, been discovering that perhaps you are not the prize you thought you were. Stress reveals your flaws.

Still others struggle with the job, the extended family or health issues. How do you let all that affect you? All these situations serve to expose the cracks in your character so that they can be taken to the cross, healed and transformed.

Life in the flesh brings turmoil, while peace, stability and joy flow from the Spirit of God in the nature and character of Jesus. Because we have a hope that transcends this earth, what anyone else would see as disaster works blessing for us because God in His incredible love uses it to make us lovers, people of integrity, standing in victory and joy in the midst of the rubble of the world.

More Than Outward Behavior

Jesus did not die on a cross just to forgive us, to simply wipe away our guilt or just to give us a theology to believe in, build our lives around and be religious about. More than commandments to obey, He gave us His own nature and character to live.

As sons and daughters of God, our destiny goes well beyond mere outward behavior. God grants us wholeness from the inside out. We are not simply going to heaven one day when we die. Rather, our salvation begins here and now as transformation takes root and wholeness grows.

Past generations interpreted holiness as a list of "don'ts." Don't play cards. Don't dance. Don't drink. Don't smoke. Don't have sex outside of marriage. None of these prohibitions is wrong in itself, but neither does abstaining from these things really change the heart. When wholeness flows from the inner person, from character formation at a foundational level, it shapes outward behavior. "If by the Spirit you are putting to death the deeds of the body" (Romans 8:13) the whole world receives blessing.

The Prophetic Word

God has long been preparing a "last days" generation to emerge in the midst of this rapidly decaying world, a people who can genuinely be called the sons and daughters of God. If this generation had been evident in Paul's day, he would not have spoken of the anxious longing of the creation for them yet to be revealed. I, therefore, believe that the apostle foresaw and longed for the time in which we now live.

Throughout Church history individual believers here and there have been transformed and have stood forth as sons and daughters of God. We dubbed them "saints" and thought them to be more "special" than the rest of us. While the Church has always had such people in its midst, I know that something greater is at hand, more than just one here and another there that the world later calls "saints," or even a small group of people here and another group there. Paul spoke of a generation, a righteous and significant remnant.

God has been carefully preparing you and me to be the generation the apostle foresaw, although I am under no delusions that all of us who call ourselves believers have actually responded or will ultimately respond to the invitation. Decades ago, with preparation in mind, the Lord sent the revelation we call "inner healing" as a tool for foundational character change. In various places He has raised up ministries of transformation, not just to make us happy or to set us free, but to bring about the kind of wholeness that would more perfectly reflect His own nature.

111

Not every theology or method of inner healing has been pure and sound theologically or methodologically. Much has been foolishness. Too many people have received it, not as a tool for taking brokenness to the cross to be transformed into the image of Jesus, but as a self-centered means of attaining self-centered happiness.

In spite of all this, the effect has been life-changing for those willing to embrace the cross, to put to death the deeds of the flesh and really learn to live. Every obstacle, disaster or setback you and I have experienced has been allowed by God for just one purpose—to expose in us what does not yet look like Jesus so that it can be brought to the cross and transformed. Through all of it runs God's sovereign purpose so that one day He can reveal His work in us to the world and show off His children in pride and joy as they walk in love, in integrity and in power to vindicate His name. That day dawns now.

As the world rushes toward the climax of history and the cataclysmic end of all things, we will see the fulfillment of the prophecy of the revealing of the generation of the sons of God for which the whole of creation has longed all this time. Like the biblical leaven in the lump, these will quietly wield the power of God in signs and wonders to heal and save the multitudes who will cry out to God as the world disintegrates around them.

Concealment

The fact that something must be revealed means that something has been concealed. This generation has, therefore, been prepared in hiddenness. Perhaps you have felt held back and have wondered why. Prophecies spoken over you and senses you had for your future have been delayed and then delayed again. Because of this your hope has suffered. "Hope deferred makes the heart sick, but desire fulfilled is a tree of life" (Proverbs 13:12). In the face of extended delay, many of us have grown sick at heart, but the release of life will now come quickly. In love and for our own protection God has kept this generation hidden, out of the public eye, while He worked His transformation in us, but the time of revealing is now upon us.

Exposure

In order to reveal the good, God must expose and sort out the bad. As a prelude to the revealing of the sons and daughters of God, therefore, we have seen the exposure of sin on an international scale both in and out of the Body of Christ.

News of top executives forced to resign due to immorality and lapses of integrity seems to break weekly. I weary of watching top Christian leaders fall, one after another, caught in sexual scandals or misuse of ministry funds. Many of these have, in various ways, gone on record as refusing the tools God has given for transformation. Many of them were vocal critics of inner healing. Now they pay the price for their blindness. Judgment has begun with the house of God.

We witnessed these exposures in the national and international news beginning in the 1980s when the news broke that Jim Bakker, the biggest evangelist on television, had been involved in sexual compromise and illegal financial dealings. Jimmy Swaggart, the most well-known preacher in the world during the same era, made a tearful spectacle of himself after being caught twice with prostitutes. Paul Cain, at one time the most respected name in the prophetic movement, underwent a restoration process after being exposed in immorality. In more recent years the Body of Christ suffered the exposure of Todd Bentley's adultery at the height of the Lakeland Revival that he led. Ted Haggard, once the president of the National Association of Evangelicals, suffered exposure of his sexual compromises. In Atlanta, Eddie Long, pastor of a mega-church, privately settled a lawsuit brought by several young men alleging sexual abuse.

To their everlasting credit, some of these leaders sought help and submitted to restoration processes.

This represents only a few of the scandals that have broken in recent years. Anointing has never been and never will be a measure of holiness or wholeness. It has never been and never will be the mark of God's approval. It has only ever been the evidence of His love for the people the anointing touches. As I have said so many times, we will see many more revelations of moral compromise in days to come as the season of acceleration gathers steam and as God sorts the precious from the vile in a time leading to a renewed outbreak of glory.

Days of Ananias and Sapphira

More than twenty years ago I prophesied that the Church would one day see the return of the days of Ananias and Sapphira from Acts 5, when moral compromise under the anointing could get you killed. Ananias and Sapphira had sold some property and, seeking to gain honor for themselves, lied to the Holy Spirit concerning what portion of it they had given to the church. Peter confronted Ananias,

> "'While it remained unsold, did it not remain your own? And after it was sold, was it not under your control? Why is it that you have conceived this deed in your heart? You have not lied to men but to God.' And as he heard these words, Ananias fell down and breathed his last; and great fear came over all who heard of it."
>
> Acts 5:4–5

Why they died has always been a matter of conjecture. For lack of a better way of saying it, I believe that the veil between heaven and earth thins when God pours out His Spirit in the kind of power and love that flowed in the days following Pentecost.

With it comes God's holiness and the selflessness of Jesus. When Ananias and Sapphira introduced willful compromise and deception into the power of that flow, and turned from selfless sacrifice to the need for recognition and praise, the shock of the violation was more than their physical bodies could absorb. It would be something like going from sixty miles per hour to a dead stop in a tenth of a second, or getting clotheslined at the neck while at a dead run.

God did not kill Ananias and Sapphira and neither did the words Peter spoke to them. They died because of the shock of their own sin when introduced into the selfless flow of power in which the Church moved at that time.

Today, from leadership to the average believer, the Body of Christ is rife with such compromise. As I write, the news has broken that the pastor of a mega-church in Orlando was found dead in a New York hotel room at the age of 42. His marriage had broken up a couple of years prior due to an affair he had with an exotic dancer, and there were allegations of substance abuse. In my own church, during a time of strong outpouring of the Spirit, we saw three deaths visited upon people guilty of sowing defilement and baseless criticism into the fellowship and against leadership. Not yet even fifty years old, two of these died of sudden heart attacks, one of them with no prior cardiac history.

Take warning! As God increases His power and presence upon us, there will be less and less room for willful compromise. More than exposure, concerning which the Body of Christ seems to care little these days, the secret sinner risks tangible harm. Two dangers loom: (1) at last, weary of leaders and disciples who blaspheme His name with moral compromise while walking under the anointing, God must act to defend His own righteousness, and (2) when the flow of the Spirit and His selfless love carries the kind of power that flowed in the days following

Pentecost, the shock of violation can have a devastating effect on the physical body. Engage in moral compromise during these coming days and you may endanger your very life. Barring a massive move of repentance, we will see more sudden deaths as this season unfolds.

Convergence of Character and Anointing

We are now entering a time when anointing and the nature of Jesus in those who minister the Kingdom must converge so that we see true sons and daughters of God walking simultaneously in His character and in supernatural power. As God sorts out the bad we will see a revealing of the good, those who have been held back while God has made character changes and brought about real transformation.

A new generation of leadership is emerging to lead a fresh generation of the Body of Christ who will shine with His nature. Signs and wonders, power ministry and healings will follow after those the Lord reveals as those who have come to look like Him, carrying the Father's heart, but the focus of their lives will not fall on the supernatural. Real holiness and genuine supernatural power flow inside out from godly wholeness that results in the kind of intimacy with God that Jesus spoke of when He said that He and the Father were one. Inner change produces outward action and consistently good fruit.

Essential Humility

The rise of an elite group standing above everyone else in hubristic pride was not what Paul had in mind when he predicted the revealing of the sons of God in Romans 8:19. Rather, he foresaw the day when a righteous generation of the Body of Christ would arise to impact the world, prepared and shaped by God's own hand to vindicate His name and to reap a harvest of souls in love and in power in the last days. When Jesus calls, the true sons and daughters of God hear and embrace the changes He sends to conform them to His own image. Elitism disqualifies. Humility opens the way. "God is opposed to the proud, but gives grace to the humble" (James 4:6).

God's hand produces the kind of humble heart that the apostle Paul wrote of when he confessed his unworthiness to be called an apostle because he had persecuted the Church (see 1 Corinthians 15:9), even as signs and wonders followed after him. Again in Romans 7 he bared his soul as a sinner needing deliverance. Some think Paul spoke of the days before his conversion, but he wrote in the present tense, humbly revealing his ongoing struggle, before revealing the solution in Romans 8. Yet again in 2 Corinthians 12 he boasted, not of his strength, but of his weakness, and then demonstrated humility by embracing that weakness as the means through which God could more perfectly manifest His power. I speak therefore of a rising generation of disciples walking simply and humbly, unimpressed with themselves and filled with the wonder of Jesus our Lord. God will grant them power for signs and wonders, as well as increasing influence in the Church and in the world, because in humility they will not need power.

The Right to Become

"But as many as received Him, to them He gave the right to become children of God, even to those who believe in His name, who were born, not of blood nor of the will of the flesh nor of the will of man, but of God" (John 1:12–13). Notice John's choice of words: "the right to become." Just because you said a prayer and supposedly received Him does not make you a "son (or daughter) of God." In the same way that every American citizen has the right to vote, but until you exercise that right it will do no one any good, at your salvation you received a right that must be exercised before it can become a reality. We have been saved by grace as a free gift, but godly character must be chosen and embraced. Before you count yourself a part of this godly generation, be certain of your choices.

The apostle Paul exhorted the Philippians to "prove yourselves to be blameless and innocent, children of God above reproach in the midst of a crooked and perverse generation, among whom you appear as lights in the world" (Philippians 2:15). Note the clear references to character. We must choose to be blameless, innocent and above reproach in the midst of a twisted and decaying world. Salvation is a gift, but character is a choice.

"See how great a love the Father has bestowed on us, that we would be called children of God; and such we are" (1 John 3:1). Connect this with 1 John 2:29: "If you know that He is righteous, you know that everyone also who practices righteousness is born of Him." John understood that character must be chosen, pursued and practiced.

Conclusion

The judgment cycle (Greek *krisis*) of exposure of unrighteousness and faulty character will soon run its course. Not long from now a hidden generation will be revealed to the world who have been steeped, not primarily in power or even in supernatural experience, but in wholeness and character formation. Because of what they have become in Him, these will vindicate His name, redeem the tarnished image of a compromising and self-centered Church before the world and minister in greater power than any generation before them. God is about to show off this emerging generation as His handiwork.

Many in my nation and around the world have been called of God to be part of this. I meet them every time I travel to speak.

All of them share the same testimony of never really fitting in with what seems to be the predominant stream. Exhibiting a deep sense of humility, they testify to their hunger for a simple and uncomplicated intimacy with God. They have been carefully concealed until they no longer need to be seen by others, to stand on anyone's stage or to hear their names spoken with reverence and admiration. They have been changed and now carry an air of humility that contributes to a sense of power about to be released. Watch for the shift in leadership and in the tone and feel of the River of God over the next few years. The recycled Baalism of our day has no power over these.

8

THE FINAL INVITATION: REVELATION 14

Then I looked, and behold, the Lamb was standing on Mount Zion, and with Him one hundred and forty-four thousand, having His name and the name of His Father written on their foreheads.

Revelation 14:1

Avariety of interpretations have been set forth for the identity of the 144,000 in the book of Revelation from chapter 7 and chapter 14. Lacking an understanding of biblical symbolism, awareness of the nature of apocalyptic literature and a sense of history, most miss the mark. Because this is not the place to debate the merits of the various views of the identity of the 144,000, I will limit myself to stating what I know to be true.

Based on the description of their nature here in Revelation 14, I believe the 144,000 to be the same group whose rise Paul prophesied in Romans 8—the sons and daughters of God revealed in the last days. Unfortunately, deeply compromised and woefully unprepared, the majority of the Body of Christ in our time cannot be described in this way. Like Paul, John saw in his visions an end time group of believers, a definite minority, who would refuse compromise in any form. He foresaw a people who would seek holiness and wholeness in order to be dramatically transformed to conform to the image of Jesus. Not that they would be perfect. Perfection can only happen when Jesus changes us in the twinkling of an eye at the last trumpet when He returns. This does, however, point to a generation making firm decisions for the shape and direction of their lives.

In Revelation 14 John contrasted two groups, one destined to be gathered to the Lord at the last day in what many call the Rapture, and the other destined for wrath and hell. Because he wrote the Revelation with the history of the first and second centuries under the Roman Empire as the backdrop, this differentiation between the two groups stood out clearly in John's day. We are seeing the same thing in our own time, but it carries an end time urgency. In other words, John's words found fulfillment in the first two centuries A.D., but a foreshadowing of something greater yet to come flowed through his visions. That time is now and it calls for decision. Where will you stand? With which group will you identify?

The Symbolism of the 144,000

Apocalyptic literature like the book of Revelation cannot be called prophecy in the usual sense. While prophecy is spoken, apocalyptic words are written. While prophecy delivers a very direct message from the Lord concerning the present, the future and the distant future, apocalyptic words address the same thing in the form of visions and dreams. For this reason the language and imagery of apocalyptic words exhibit a fluid quality. As in any dream, in apocalyptic literature sounds and images can be both hard and soft, bright and dark, harsh and gentle all at the same time. In the same way that the meaning of dreams and visions comes cloaked in symbolism needing interpretation, so does apocalyptic literature.

The Number

"Then I looked, and behold, the Lamb was standing on Mount Zion, and with Him one hundred and forty-four thousand, having His name and the name of His Father written on their foreheads" (14:1).

The number 144 results from multiplying twelve times twelve, which stands for the twelve patriarchs or tribes of Israel and the twelve apostles of the New Testament. The "thousand" part of it symbolically indicates not a specific number, but an indeterminate large number of people. Together this represents the makeup of the whole Body of Christ, both Jewish and Gentile followers of Jesus, a group of people devoted to the Lord in wholeness of character, as we shall see in the following verses. This same group first appeared in 7:3–4 where they were sealed on the forehead to protect against the plagues and torments to come upon the earth.

Written on Their Foreheads

To mark ownership, the Romans often branded slaves on the forehead. Symbolically, in imagery drawn from the culture in which John and the early Church lived, this end time body of believers has been branded as "slaves" of Jesus and the Father. This sounds very much like Paul's "sons of God" (see Romans 8:19) to be revealed at the last day. These people know themselves to be wholly owned, completely sold out to

God. They brook no compromise and understand that slaves have neither freedoms nor choices. In the face of all opposition they walk the true walk. As purchased properties bought by the precious blood of Jesus, these know that complete obedience to Him is the only true freedom and that everything else constitutes slavery.

Slaves have no rights. How many Christians today have failed to understand that when we came to Jesus we surrendered our rights? We are not our own. Because we have been branded as belonging to the Lord, we have neither the right nor the freedom to do with our bodies or our lives what we choose to do. Most of the Body of Christ does not yet fully understand this, and this deficit constitutes a key reason the Church stands unprepared for what must soon come upon the world. Just one right remains to us, the exercise of which is the gateway to freedom and glory. "But as many as received Him, to them He gave the right to become children of God" (John 1:12). If we choose to exercise it, we have a right to become just like Jesus. The true name of this slavery is freedom and therein lies one of the essential paradoxes of our faith.

On Mount Zion

In the Old Testament God chose Mount Zion, the hill on which Jerusalem sits, as the place of His presence (see Psalm 43:3 and others). Because this word comes couched in symbolic dream imagery, John did not intend for us to look for a literal 144,000 believers all crowded on the top of that literal hill. He meant us to understand that these wholly owned end time believers would stand in the raw and immediate presence of God with Jesus at the center. These have sought intimacy with Him as a focused and singular goal and been changed by it. The tangible sense of God's presence has become their home wherever they go.

A Sound from Heaven

> And I heard a voice from heaven, like the sound of many waters and like the sound of loud thunder, and the voice which I heard was like the sound of harpists playing on their harps. And they sang a new song before the throne and before the four living creatures and the elders; and no one could learn the song except the one hundred and forty-four thousand who had been purchased from the earth.
>
> Revelation 14:2–3

Here we see the fluidity of the imagery of visions and dreams expressed in a sound both loud like thunder and delicate as the plucking of a chorus of harps, at the same time overpowering and gentle, forceful and soft, shaking and comforting. John heard the voices of the many sounding as one, indicating worship offered in the power of wondrous unity.

God summons us to be that generation now, offering up worship infused with all the qualities of God's presence in reflection of His nature. It is not entertainment. In these last days, worship among the wholly owned will grow in power as well as the gentle touch, the roar as well as the whisper and thunderous proclamation as well as sweet comfort. A new pulse of worship has already broken forth that can flow only from the sold-out, 100 percent laid down lovers of God. As a "sound from heaven" this worship originates in the supernatural and manifests on earth.

> And they sang a new song before the throne and before the four living creatures and the elders; and no one could learn the song except the one hundred and forty-four thousand who had been purchased from the earth.
>
> Revelation 14:3

As worship takes on new force and power for the sons and daughters of God in these last days—our day—it carries a quality of uniqueness and even urgency.

Here we find that not everyone can enter into this kind of worship and in effect "learn" it because it can only flow from and be truly felt by those who have been branded as wholly owned. It rises from a place in the heart that has been profoundly changed, a place that has come to look like Him, so that it resonates powerfully with the Spirit of Jesus.

A worship revival is coming in these last days, a "song" that the compromisers and the lukewarm cannot learn because it comes exclusively from undivided hearts. Others will hear it, sense the presence of God in it and be drawn by it, but will not be able to comprehend its depth or power without making the sacrifice the true sons and daughters of God have made. This worship revival has already begun and the invitation has gone out to make the decisions that lead to the fullness of this gift.

As this new wave of worship breaks upon those who can learn the song and enter in, we will see a dramatic rise in sovereign signs and wonders poured out in the context of worship in congregations I have called "lighthouse churches." Increasingly, God will touch His children with healing power in the context of worship without the mediation of any human agent. Already, in some places, this has begun to manifest. In my own church over the last couple of years we have seen a number of people healed by the sovereign touch of God during the course of powerful worship when no one was praying for them. This kind of manifestation will become increasingly common in lighthouse congregations over the course of the next five to ten years.

Once more, however, I must emphasize that this surge of freshly anointed worship will not be for the lukewarm. We will not see sovereign signs and wonders like this in the so-called seeker-sensitive churches where the move of God is limited and where lukewarm and less than radical commitment is tolerated in the name of not alienating anyone. To cop a phrase from Jesus' language, "the time is coming and now is" when nothing less than radical commitment and the kind of extended and passionate worship that brings the Presence will be enough to satisfy the needs of those crying out for help in a desperate time. A great redeployment of the sheep is coming as those who seek the genuine begin to learn where to find it.

The verse ends by saying that these 144,000, Paul's "sons of God," have been "purchased from the earth," meaning they have been bought by the blood of Jesus and are therefore no longer citizens of this earth and its culture. Paid for and owned, they have been marked as belonging to Him.

Essence of Character

> These are the ones who have not been defiled with women, for they have kept themselves chaste. These are the ones who follow the Lamb wherever He goes. These have been purchased from among men as first fruits to God and to the Lamb. And no lie was found in their mouth; they are blameless.
>
> Revelation 14:4–5

Undefiled

We have lived in a time of extended grace when God seemed to pour out His blessing and His power through some deeply compromised vessels. As this era comes to a close, however, the patience of God wears thin. We are now transitioning from the age of exposure and warning into the age of judgment. In the coming days, the ones who wield the power of God with anything less than integrity expose themselves to danger. God cannot long permit His name to be blasphemed.

Thus the generation of the sons and daughters of God, the 144,000 (symbolic number) here in Revelation 14, walk before the Lord in purity of heart. One evidence of the symbolic nature of the number can be seen in the words "have not defiled themselves with women." How silly would it be to assume that the 144,000 were only men? More important, God declares sex between a man and woman married to one another to be holy. It only becomes unholy and defiling when engaged in outside of that covenant relationship. Therein lies the symbolism.

In both the Old and New Testaments, God relates to His people as to a bride. As such He demands and deserves faithfulness to the marriage covenant we share with Him. For this reason, adultery, fornication and harlotry became the paradigm for Israel's unfaithfulness, immorality and idolatrous practices. For example:

> And I saw that for all the adulteries of faithless Israel, I had sent her away and given her a writ of divorce, yet her treacherous sister Judah did not fear; but she went and was a harlot also. Because of the lightness of her harlotry, she polluted the land and committed adultery with stones and trees.
>
> Jeremiah 3:8–9

In short, the symbolism of this verse—and many others like it—points to compromised devotion to God.

Harlotry is the Bible's word for prostitution. In other words, sin and compromise offer a reward; otherwise there would be no appeal. The fertility gods that seduced Israel offered payment for their services in the form of the promise of prosperity, luring them into a focus on self, compromise and immorality at the expense of devotion to God. It ended in judgment and destruction. Nothing has changed. We sin today for the promise of some positive or pleasing return, which might last for a moment, but ultimately betrays its promise. Defilement and destruction result, as well as broken covenant and shattered relationship with God. Sin offers a reward it cannot deliver.

In falling to its deception we join the Baal-influenced culture around us, entering into the worship of the demon. We buy in to its values and attitudes for the sake of a promised reward that results in delusion and defilement. Sexual sin, for instance, offers a self-centered reward in pleasure and in love but results in a loss of glory and a broken capacity to truly bond in covenant. Or when tempted to lie, the lie offers protection, but imprisons the liar in a web of destruction that defiles and robs everyone it touches.

For the sake of His own name, in days to come our Lord will move to put a stop to compromised integrity and will defend the holiness of His name, beginning with leadership. If we cannot learn concern for integrity through witnessing the warning brought by exposure of sin in top leadership, then the lesson will be driven home through the actual deaths we will see. Believe it or not, this is mercy and love for all concerned that the many might be warned and saved through the discipline of the few. "Those who continue in sin, rebuke in the presence of all, so that the rest also will be fearful of sinning" (1 Timothy 5:20).

Chastity Defined

John defined chastity for the sons of God with the words "they follow the Lamb wherever He goes." In symbolism this speaks of absolute obedience and singularity of devotion. The first twelve disciples understood it when they left everything—a lucrative fishing business, tax collecting and so on—to follow Jesus without condition, not even knowing where they were going. Imagine being sent out on a missionary journey some time later with no change of clothes, no money and no shoes. Obedience means following and obeying fully even when you cannot see the road ahead.

128

This generation of sold-out followers of Jesus have learned the glory and blessing of complete obedience. Established and settled character brooks no compromise, no pet sin tolerated and regarded as minor, and bears the fruit of glory, joy and fulfillment. Unlike sin, righteousness delivers on its promises. The wholly owned know this and the fire of it consumes them. Many of those mired in this culture, steeped in compromise, will soon be looking for a way out as the inevitable suffering mounts and they discover that sin does not work. The sold-out will be there to provide the answer.

No Lie in Their Mouths

Nothing less than absolute integrity in the minutest of issues will do in these coming days. I have heard eyewitness accounts of pastors from foreign countries attending the Lakeland Revival in Florida who bought expensive items from stores. In order to avoid paying duties and taxes when they returned to their own countries, they convinced the clerks to write up false invoices showing lower purchase prices. Unacceptable! The sons of God, the wholly owned ones, understand the price of compromise at any level and make appropriate choices.

Inclusion in the company of those who experience the raw presence of God and participate in the glory of supernatural worship will not be granted to those who fail to understand this. They will not be counted among the revealed sons and daughters of God who walk with the Lord in intimacy and glory. Lest the full harvest be defiled, firstfruits cannot be rotten fruit. Unfortunately we have become a predominantly lukewarm Body of Christ in America and the West. At this time in history, grace for this kind of behavior has run out. Some think to wait until the last minute to get their lives and integrity in order, but because sin kills they are storing up destruction for themselves. We no longer have the luxury of time.

The Harvest to Come

> And I saw another angel flying in midheaven, having an eternal gospel to preach to those who live on the earth, and to every nation and tribe and tongue and people; and he said with a loud voice, "Fear God, and give Him glory, because the hour of His judgment has come; worship Him who made the heaven and the earth and sea and springs of waters."
>
> Revelation 14:6–7

The language echoes that of Matthew 24:14: "This gospel of the kingdom shall be preached in the whole world as a testimony to all the nations, and then the end will come."

At its core, the Great Apostasy of the last days is nothing more than a separation of the wheat from the chaff. Some will fall away while the true and righteous stand their ground. In the time prior to the Rapture of the saints prophesied in the last verses of this chapter, those who remain will bring in a harvest of souls unprecedented in history.

In the mid-1970s, my seminary years, I was told that 25,000 unreached people groups remained on earth. A decade ago that number had been reduced to 3,000. Recently, friends of mine involved in missions informed me that the number remaining has been reduced to 200 and that these have been strategically targeted. In Toronto, in October 2011, I heard Wes Hall of the International House of Prayer say that according to information he had received, by November 2011 every people group on the planet with more than 10,000 people will have a Christian witness in its midst.

This is the day of the final call that originates in heaven and manifests on earth as we near the goal of reaching every tribe, tongue and nation. No time remains for games and compromises. Heaven itself has initiated a renewed push to save as many as possible before the Lord's return. The godly ones John foresaw in this chapter and that Paul wrote of in Romans 8 stand forth as firstfruits of the great end time harvest of souls already breaking out in the world everywhere except the nations of the West. As Western society inevitably collapses, however, the West will be next in line for a Holy Spirit outpouring as desperate sinners—those who have an ear to hear—cry out for answers.

The Fall of Babylon

"And another angel, a second one, followed, saying, 'Fallen, fallen is Babylon the great, she who has made all the nations drink of the wine of the passion of her immorality'" (14:8). In 586 B.C. Babylon conquered Judah and destroyed Jerusalem. In order to prevent rebellion, they carried the cream of the population into exile. There the people faced strong pressure to conform to the culture of Babylon and to worship its gods. In this way Babylon became a paradigm for any oppressive and immoral society pressuring and seducing the people of God to compromise.

In the context of Revelation, Babylon is the Roman Empire of John's day, but the prophecy foreshadows something greater for a later time immediately prior to the Lord's return. Not only has the culture of the Western world infiltrated and seduced the Church into compromise and acceptance of immorality and false doctrine, but it has developed in a way that has become actively hostile toward those of us who stand on the Word of God and refuse to call evil good and good evil.

We have only just begun to see the level of hatred that will be directed against us who stand the ground for morality and faith, even as we win many out of the world to Jesus. Some will understand that we refuse to accept sin because sin does not work. Sin makes you stupid. Sin kills. Even so, the culture and many nations of the world increasingly consider us a dangerous threat, just as they did in John's day.

The world as we have known it verges on collapse. God's promise to Christians under Roman domination and to us in our day was and is that this evil culture must fail and fall, just as both Babylon and Rome eventually did. In the midst of that collapse, the righteous will stand forth and a harvest of souls will be reaped. In John's day Rome "fell" to the Christians, then disintegrated as an empire. Something similar is taking shape in our day as we gather a harvest of souls in the midst of the disintegration of the societies and nations in which we live. We must be ready and, as I have said before, the Church as a whole is not even close. Let the sons and daughters of God arise and stand forth!

The Beast and His Mark

> Then another angel, a third one, followed them, saying with a loud voice, "If anyone worships the beast and his image, and receives a mark on his forehead or on his hand, he also will drink of the wine of the wrath of God, which is mixed in full strength in the cup of His anger; and he will be tormented with fire and brimstone in the presence of the holy angels and in the presence of the Lamb."
>
> Revelation 14:9–10

We need to lose the silly teaching going around about electronic chips embedded in our bodies and tattoos marked on our skin. This is all merely symbolism. In the same way that Jesus will not literally brand believers on the forehead, neither will the mark of the beast be a physical mark. Apocalyptic literature is dream language, not a literal representation.

Emperor worship took root in the Roman Empire as an outpouring of gratitude for the Pax Romana, the peace that Rome imposed over the entire Mediterranean region. It brought unprecedented prosperity by freeing trade from the threat of pirates and brigands and by building roads all over the empire. The beast represents the system of emperor worship and veneration of the gods of Rome that arose as an outpouring of gratitude and eventually became all but compulsory. To receive the "mark" meant that you had compromised your Christian commitment by participating in these pagan rituals.

Revelation 13:17 speaks of not being able to buy or sell without the mark of the beast. Historically this had much to do with the requirement in many Roman cities that in order to practice a trade one had to belong to a trade guild. Dedicated to various Roman gods, the guilds met in the temples of those gods where they offered sacrifice and held feasts that often ended in orgies—shades of Babylon. Needless to say, in order to make a living, Christians found themselves strongly tempted to participate.

The mark, therefore, symbolically represents compromise and a declaration of loyalty. To what or to whom do you really belong? When the pressure is on, will you compromise your commitment as a Christian to get along in the world? Do you keep silent about your faith just to keep your job? Under the pressure of the Baal spirit, have you joined the world's way of thinking concerning morality, right and wrong, or do you stand your ground at any cost? Increasingly, Christians can be economically penalized for taking Jesus to work and refusing to participate in practices that are less than ethical.

John drew his symbolism from Deuteronomy 6:6–8:

> These words, which I am commanding you today, shall be on your heart. You shall teach them diligently to your sons and shall talk of them when you sit in your house and when you walk by the way and when you lie down and when you rise up. You shall bind them as a sign on your hand and they shall be as frontals on your forehead.

133

From that time to this, every orthodox Jew obeys this command literally by binding phylacteries—little leather boxes containing Scripture—on their hands and foreheads in a daily ritual. The mark of the beast is not a literal or visible thing, but rather a symbolic representation of a declaration of loyalty to the world system as evidenced by compromise with its ungodly values and practices.

The Reality of Hell

"And the smoke of their torment goes up forever and ever; they have no rest day and night, those who worship the beast and his image, and whoever receives the mark of his name" (14:11). Regardless of the confession of their lips, those who give their loyalty to the beast of the devil-inspired world system face a terrifying future. Hell is real.

"Here is the perseverance of the saints who keep the commandments of God and their faith in Jesus" (14:12). Persecution will increase in the days to come, up to and including death, even in the so-called tolerant Western world, as will the seductive lure of ungodly societal attitudes and beliefs. Under pervasive pressure to compromise, to despair, to cave in, to live for self, we must stand our ground. I cry out for the Lord's people to make the choices necessary to be included in the end time company of the sons of God revealed and to participate in its glory and power. The early Church won. So will we. Over us, Baal must have no influence.

9

SIGNS OF THE BAAL SPIRIT

I f I have not yet convinced you of the pervasive influence of Baal on the culture of the Western world, consider the following. I travel internationally as a conference speaker in renewal circles, and nearly everywhere I go I feel a blanket of suppression over the assemblies. In almost every meeting I sense a great deal more power present than the people appear to be receiving. In some this can be attributed to an unwillingness to fully surrender and allow God to have His way. In others it feels like spiritual slumber or even a functional inability to receive, often in spite of a strong desire to encounter God.

I remember the freedom we experienced in the early years of the Toronto outpouring, when the freshness of that move of the Spirit swept nearly everyone up in its joy and innocence. In those days we needed neither method nor teaching to tell us how to do things. Under the anointing, with a kind of youthful exuberance, we prayed for the sick without the need to attend a four-day healing conference and carry a notebook home filled with instruction on how to pray. Wonder of wonders, the sick recovered! I personally received some of the best prophetic words of my life back then. Nothing since that time has come close. Method and knowledge have too often replaced innocence and freedom.

In too many places today we seem to be trying so very hard, in some cases behaving outwardly as though continuing to receive what we no longer really do. It seems like form without substance or a glass once filled but now half empty. Why? What has changed?

Actually, in the realm of the Holy Spirit, nothing has changed. He still comes. He always loves. He continues to pour forth His power. The only thing that has changed through the years is that Baal's influence has grown in strength and has cast a blanket of suppression over the people of God. The power of that suppression rises in direct proportion to the degree that God's people have succumbed to the influence of the Baal spirit. Most fail to realize how deeply they have been affected by the self-focus this brings and the compromises it leads us to make.

Four Marks of the Baal Spirit

The real religion of America and the West is the recycled Baalism I have already referenced, although we would never call it that. The same demon that seduced and ultimately destroyed Israel now pervasively infects and influences the culture of the Western world. This is the principality against which we struggle. "For our struggle is not against flesh and blood, but against the rulers, against the powers, against the world forces of this darkness, against the spiritual forces of wickedness in the heavenly places" (Ephesians 6:12). Baalism carries with it four clear markers, all of which are clearly in evidence in contemporary Western culture for those who have eyes to see.

1. Consuming Self-Focus

Fertility cults like the one centered around Baal focus on prosperity. Prosperity as a goal feeds a consuming self-focus and leads us to offer certain sacrifices to ensure the service of self and material success. Accordingly, the post–World War II baby boomer generation, of which I am a part, became known as the "me generation." I have already spoken of the destructive effects of this on individual lives, families and society. As it has shaped doctrines, ministries and worship styles, this focus has infected and eventually stifled every move of the Holy Spirit in my lifetime.

2. Rampant Sexual Immorality

I have already pointed out God's indictment of Israel for sexual immorality as stated by Amos. Baal worship in ancient Israel included the use of temple prostitutes as a kind of sympathetic magic to ensure the growth of crops and the multiplication of livestock. "There were also male cult prostitutes in the land. They did according to all the abominations of the nations which the LORD dispossessed before the sons of Israel" (1 Kings 14:24). "He also broke down the houses of the male cult prostitutes which were in the house of the LORD, where the women were weaving hangings for the Asherah" (2 Kings 23:7).

> I will not punish your daughters when they play the harlot or your brides when they commit adultery, for the men themselves go apart with harlots and offer sacrifices with temple prostitutes; so the people without understanding are ruined.
>
> Hosea 4:14

While people have always engaged in fornication, at one time we in the Western world at least had the moral sense to know that those who did so were doing something wrong. Today, even those who claim to believe the Scriptures treat sexual immorality as a normal thing, something to be expected when an unmarried couple "loves" one another. Nationally, the number of couples living together without benefit of marriage has increased exponentially. As I write, the majority of wedding ceremonies I have performed over the last several months have involved couples not only living together unmarried, but who have already produced children together, some as old as teenagers. This does not even begin to address the issue of homosexuality and the rise of its acceptance as a normal lifestyle.

Movies, books, television shows and magazines present sexual compromise as a normal and expected part of life and relationships. Romantic music accompanies the heavy breathing and writhing bodies to make it all seem so wonderful. Sex in marriage is indeed wonderful. By contrast, sex outside of marriage defiles and defrauds—something we seem all too willing to do in many ways and at many varied levels in this culture as we serve the idol of self.

3. Sacrifice of the Children

"For the sons of Judah have done that which is evil in My sight," declares the LORD, "they have set their detestable things in the house which is called by My name, to defile it. They have built the high places of Topheth, which is in the valley of the son of Hinnom, to burn their sons and their daughters in the fire, which I did not command, and it did not come into My mind."

Jeremiah 7:30–31

There really should be no need to point out the staggering number of children murdered in their mothers' wombs since *Roe v. Wade* (United States Supreme Court) legalized abortion on demand in 1973. *Holocaust* would be the only word to adequately describe what has happened. Sacrificed on the altar of our cultural self-absorption, the altar of Baal, their blood cries out to our Father God for justice.

4. Cutting and Self-Mutilation

In 1 Kings 18 Elijah challenged the prophets of Baal to a contest. Altars would be built and the people would know the true God as the one who sent fire from heaven. Elijah allowed the prophets of Baal to go first. "So they cried with a loud voice and cut themselves according to their custom with swords and lances until the blood gushed out on them" (1 Kings 18:28).

My son has worked with youth for a decade and a half. He tells me that one in three teenage girls cuts and I have no reason to doubt his figures. A lesser percentage of boys engage in the same kind of destruction. Most do it in places on their bodies where their parents cannot see. Some bear permanent scars. Psychologically, they do this as an outlet for a depth of emotional pain they can express in no other way. Our self-absorbed older generation has effectively abandoned them so that they have no one to talk to and no compassionate heart to come alongside and hear their cries. Although they do this to relieve psychological stresses, I see the evidence and influence of the Baal spirit behind it. When coupled with the other three signs of Baal's influence, this epidemic of cutting and self-mutilation cannot be a coincidence. Baal delights in the murder of the children and the mutilation of the young.

The Outcome of Baal's Influence

In the midst of all this compromise and acceptance of demonic ideas, mindsets and practices foreign to true faith, Israel did not believe they had abandoned God any more than many so-called Christians engaged in moral compromise do today. Having come under demonic influence, they had begun to incorporate idolatrous demonic ways into the practice of their own faith.

Every culture and nation that has succumbed to the Baal spirit has ultimately collapsed. America and the West yet have time for the people of God to do their work, to prepare themselves to reap a harvest, but during this time of preparation, cultural and societal decay will continue and accelerate. As the inevitable reaping of what has been sown, Western culture teeters on the brink of implosion in every aspect of economics, society and religion. We have little time.

We believers have been granted a period of grace—five literal years from May 2010 or a figurative indeterminate period of time—in which to prepare. Repentance and prayer can extend this season, or perhaps reverse the trend temporarily, but society as a whole will not turn. Knowingly or unknowingly, the masses will continue to follow Baal, just as Israel did so long ago. A firm decision has been made in the heart of the culture that will not be changed. A harvest of souls can and will be reaped out of the destruction we already see unfolding, but the culture around us will continue on its chosen course.

In the book of Revelation, John wrote that even in the face of devastating judgments, mankind as a whole would not turn:

> The rest of mankind, who were not killed by these plagues, did not repent of the works of their hands, so as not to worship demons, and the idols of gold and of silver and of brass and of stone and of wood, which can neither see nor hear nor walk; and they did not repent of their murders nor of their sorceries nor of their immorality nor of their thefts.
>
> Revelation 9:20–21

The dividing line between light and dark grows sharper with every passing day. We must make certain on which side of that line we stand. It is time to pray.

10

STRATEGIC PRAYER FIRE

Crucial to this period of preparation and worthy of its own chapter is prayer. A shift has occurred in the tone and shape of the prayer God calls for, as well as in heaven's response to it. Ministries like the International House of Prayer in Kansas City have pioneered this shift, prophetically pressing ahead as forerunners long before the urgency of the present day began to unfold. In this chapter you will find a prescription for the content and spirit of the prayer we must offer in this critical period of time.

The Book of Revelation

Revelation, the most difficult book of the Bible for the average believer to understand, speaks of the end times, although much of what the apostle John wrote came to pass in the first couple of centuries A.D. As I have already pointed out, first and foremost he wrote the Revelation for Christians suffering persecution under the Roman Empire.

Prophetic perspective, however, layers the present, the future and the distant future all onto one frame, making it difficult to sort out prophecies already fulfilled in history from what must yet unfold. Although the book reflects actual history, much of Revelation therefore also applies to us and tells us what to expect in the days to come.

Many have interpreted the seven churches in the beginning of the book to be seven successive church ages, but no basis can be found in good exegesis for this view. John wrote to seven actual congregations existing simultaneously in what is now Turkey and therefore addressed not a succession of church ages, but real people, his contemporaries.

Similarly, the most common view of the seven seals, the seven trumpets, the seven significant signs and the seven bowls has been to regard them as consecutive events in time. A better explanation, however, might be termed the "diamond view." In other words, each of these groups of seven symbolic elements views the same events as though they were light passing through the prism of a four-sided diamond, each refracting the same light into different colors revealing different aspects of the same thing. Each sequence of events in each of these four views ends in the same place—the return of Jesus.

A good parallel might be a telling of the history of the American Civil War, first from the perspective of a private in the Union army from 1861 to 1865. We might then rewind and begin the story again, but this time from the perspective of then-President Abraham Lincoln. A third time we might reset to 1861 and view it all through the eyes of General Robert E. Lee of the Army of Northern Virginia. Each version of the same history begins in 1861 and ends with Lee's surrender at Appomattox Courthouse in April 1865, but each story reads very differently. Thus Revelation foretells the time of the return of the Lord and the events leading up to it from the same starting point to the same ending, but from four different perspectives.

The seven seals envision a scroll rolled up and sealed down the side with seven wax seals. The opening of the scroll illuminates the return of the Lord from the perspective of the revealing and fulfillment of the Word of God. In the beginning, God spoke and the universe leaped into being. Here, His word sets events in motion that lead to the return of Jesus.

The facet of the diamond represented by the seven trumpets refracts the light of the return of Jesus through the perspective of the announcement of the coming of the King. When an ancient near eastern king approached, he sent messengers before him to sound shofars—ram's horn trumpets—to alert the people to prepare themselves for his arrival. In Revelation, the King approaches, the trumpets sound, and the sequence once more culminates in the return of the Lord.

The third facet reveals seven significant signs refracting the light of the return of the Lord from the perspective of cosmic or spiritual realities. The seven bowls follow, revealing the coming of the Lord from the perspective of God's wrath poured out on an unrepentant world.

The Interlude at Revelation 8:2–5

A curious literary interlude appears between the breaking of the seals and the blowing of the trumpets at Revelation 8:2–5. It appears to be a great pause as the story rewinds to the beginning to tell it all again from the next perspective. We today live in the period of time represented by this interlude immediately prior to the commencement of the final sequence of events leading to the Lord's return, and as history accelerates into sharpened warfare between good and evil. The dramatic intervention of God at the Lord's return must follow.

This pause quite literally represents the time in which we live, as the angels hold back the four winds that would blow destruction upon the earth and as God seals His people against the plagues to come (see Revelation 7). Above all, it is a time for prayer magnified by heaven as we stand on the threshold of the last days. This lends intense urgency to the season now upon us.

The Altar of Incense

"When the Lamb broke the seventh seal, there was silence in heaven for about half an hour" (Revelation 8:1). Everything in heaven halts to hear the prayers of the saints. Every eye and ear stops to focus on just one thing. Heaven holds its breath.

"And I saw the seven angels who stand before God, and seven trumpets were given to them" (8:2). The trumpets announce the intervention of God in history, the return of the King, but the angels hold back. They wait for the prayers of the saints, the "holy ones" who have been cleansed and made pure by the blood of Jesus, and for God's answer to those prayers. The sons and daughters of God soon to be revealed are first and foremost a praying people.

> Another angel came and stood at the altar, holding a golden censer; and much *incense was given to him, so that he might add it to the prayers of all the saints* on the golden altar which was before the throne. And the smoke of the incense, with the prayers of the saints, went up before God out of the angel's hand.
>
> Revelation 8:3–4, emphasis mine

John found himself caught up in a vision of the heavenly temple of which the earthly Tabernacle of Moses and the Temple in Jerusalem were mere pale reflections.

According to the instructions given to Moses, the altar of incense stood immediately before the holy of holies where a curtain shielded the Ark of the Covenant, the earthly symbol of the very throne of God. Exodus 30:1 says, "Moreover, you shall make an altar as a place for burning incense; you shall make it of acacia wood." Incense symbolizes prayer rising to the Lord as a pleasing aroma to Him. "Its length shall be a cubit, and its width a cubit, it shall be square, and its height shall be two cubits; its horns shall be of one piece with it" (30:2). This meant that the altar of incense stood approximately three feet high and a foot and a half square, or approximately a meter high and half a meter square. A low railing around the top kept the incense and ashes from falling out while a horn-shaped decoration accented each corner.

God further instructed Moses to overlay it with gold and outfit it with rings and poles for transport and then continued: "You shall put this altar in front of the veil that is near the ark of the testimony, in front of the mercy seat that is over the ark of the testimony, where I will meet with you" (30:6). The ark symbolized His presence. Through prayer we enter that presence. This entire scene therefore indicates intimate prayer in the very presence of God. We live now in a Kingdom season requiring intensified and urgent prayer in preparation for the troubles to come as the time of the Lord's return approaches.

"You shall not offer any strange incense on this altar, or burnt offering or meal offering; and you shall not pour out a drink offering on it" (30:9). Incense for the altar of incense was made according to a particular formula that could not be used anywhere else. Similarly, no other kind of incense made from any other formula could be burned on that altar.

During this season of the interlude prior to the final sequence, therefore, we must pray the way God commands prayer, according to His will and in tune with His wishes. Understanding His heart, we must pray in tune with His heart. Otherwise, our prayers will be offensive and inappropriate. Prayer in this season cannot be focused on us, our personal needs or our individual desires. Because no prayer other than that which reflects His heart and His desires will be accepted during this strategic time, we must seek intimacy with God and death of self as we never have before. One of the often-missed reasons for God's desire to revive and refine the prophetic movement is not to predict the future so much as to discern the heart of God and to inform the Body of Christ how to pray accordingly.

"Aaron shall make atonement on its horns once a year; he shall make atonement on it with the blood of the sin offering of atonement once a year throughout your generations. It is most holy to the LORD" (30:10). Repentance and forgiveness were included in the prayers from time to time in order to keep them pure. The prayer called for in Revelation 8 must therefore include an element of cleansing, times of deep repentance and heartfelt brokenness. The contemporary Church desperately and urgently needs a movement of repentance and brokenness. Let those of us who understand cry out for it. Without repentance and brokenness there can be no wholeness, and without wholeness there can no revealing of the sons and daughters of God.

The Nature of Our Prayers

"Then the angel took the censer and filled it with the fire of the altar, and threw it to the earth; and there followed peals of thunder and sounds and flashes of lightning and an earthquake" (Revelation 8:5). The angel casts fire from the altar of incense into the earth in response to the prayers of the saints, believers like you and me. In this season of intensification and acceleration, heaven magnifies our prayers, increasing the power of the intercession of the saints offered on earth.

Many commentators see this as the fire of vengeance and judgment cast into the earth upon those who persecute believers. They believe that the prayers of the saints in Revelation

8:2–5 petition God to send vengeance upon those who harmed them. This fits no command our Lord ever gave us to love our enemies and to bless and pray for them. For this to be the fire of judgment would contradict everything the Lord taught us concerning our role on earth.

John first wrote the Revelation for believers suffering persecution in the Roman Empire. Because John set the Revelation against the backdrop of the experience of the people to whom he wrote, much of it applies only indirectly to the future as we draw lessons from what has already taken place in history. The early Christians under persecution conquered the Roman Empire by leading many thousands of people to Jesus through love and by becoming so known for their love that in 314 A.D. the emperor Constantine declared himself and the entire empire to be Christian.

History and the teaching of Jesus taken together mean that these prayers in Revelation 8 cannot be petitions for vengeance or judgment. Likewise, the fire cast into the earth in response to these prayers cannot be the fire of destruction, but rather the "fire of the altar," prayer fire, fire that comes from prayer, fire that energizes prayer and fire that comes from the kind of intimacy with God that the altar of incense represents.

The Symbolism of Fire in the Old Testament

Fire in the Old Testament sometimes meant that God had accepted or received a sacrifice as when Elijah confronted the 450 prophets of Baal and challenged them to call fire from heaven (see 1 Kings 18). All day they danced around and cut themselves to no avail. Elijah then built an altar of stones, placed the sacrifice upon it, wet it all down three times and cried out to God. Fire came from heaven to consume it all as God received the sacrifice.

This fire in Revelation therefore means that God has heard and received the prayers of the saints. The angel adding the incense of heaven to it means that the power of this prayer has been magnified as it rises to God. During this season in which we live, heaven empowers the prayers we offer and causes that power to impact our lives and ministries on earth.

Fire came down from heaven at the consecration of Solomon's Temple.

Fire describes God's glory (see Daniel 7:9), symbolizes His holiness (see Isaiah 33:14) and stands for His protection over His people (see 2 Kings 6:17; Zechariah 2:5).

First and foremost, in Old Testament times fire symbolized God Himself. He appeared to Moses in the burning bush. When He showed Himself among the Hebrew people after they left Egypt, He guided them by fire at night and smoke by day.

The Symbolism of Fire in the New Testament

The fire cast into the earth in Revelation 8 in response to the prayers of the saints cannot be the fire of judgment because Jesus never taught us to cry for judgment. In fact, when the disciples asked if they could call for fire to come and consume those in Samaria who would not receive Jesus, He replied, "You do not know what kind of spirit you are of" (Luke 9:55).

He taught us to pray for the coming of the Kingdom of God, for His presence to fill the earth and for His will to be done here. When the disciples requested that He teach them to pray, He said, "Your kingdom come. Your will be done, on earth as it is in heaven" (Matthew 6:10). The fire cast into the earth in Revelation in response to prayer must therefore be the fire of His presence and anointing, the coming of the Kingdom of God. We live in a time of acceleration and intensification in Kingdom things, of signs and wonders in the expression of His love in accord with the rule of the Kingdom of God.

"As for me, I baptize you with water for repentance, but He who is coming after me is mightier than I, and I am not fit to remove His sandals; He will baptize you with the Holy Spirit and fire" (Matthew 3:11).

"I have come to cast fire upon the earth; and how I wish it were already kindled!" (Luke 12:49).

"And there appeared to them tongues as of fire distributing themselves, and they rested on each one of them. And they were all filled with the Holy Spirit and began to speak with other tongues, as the Spirit was giving them utterance" (Acts 2:3–4).

"And when He again brings the firstborn into the world, He says, 'And let all the angels of God worship Him.' And of the angels He says, 'Who makes His angels winds, and His ministers a flame of fire'" (Hebrews 1:6–7).

"Therefore, since we receive a kingdom which cannot be shaken, let us show gratitude, by which we may offer to God an acceptable service with reverence and awe; for our God is a consuming fire" (Hebrews 12:28–29). We receive a Kingdom from the One who is a consuming fire.

The fire cast into the earth in answer to the prayers of the saints in Revelation must therefore be the same kind of fire that fell on the Day of Pentecost when three thousand men with their families came to Jesus. This fire burns in us who receive it in this strategic time to carry us beyond ourselves into the world to set others aflame. This fire saves lives and heals the broken by the hand of God. This is Kingdom fire and it represents the greatest outpouring of the Spirit of God since the Day of Pentecost. It comes in response to the prayers of the saints magnified in heaven.

Summary and Application

We stand on the threshold of the last days during an interval in time just before the angels blow the seven trumpets and the disaster of judgment really begins to fall. It is a time for prayer, strategic prayer for a strategic time, a time when our prayers will be amplified by the very angels of heaven. Expect an escalating sense of power and presence on prayer meetings that once seemed lifeless, routine or boring.

We have been granted a five-year window of grace, literally or symbolically, corresponding to the Revelation 8:2–5 window that really opened wide sometime prior to May of 2010. We have been gifted with five years of grace for Kingdom preparation so that we might bear the weight of glory poured out on us in a darkening day. At the heart of this time of preparation stands prayer with an eschatological edge to it.

Prayer in this preparatory window of time and beyond will be prayer the likes of which we have never known before as the angel adds heavenly incense to it. Heaven will respond with Kingdom fire, fire from the very altar of God. This fire of the Kingdom of God brings more than just miracles, healings, deliverance or even raising the dead. It brings more than merely winning people to Jesus. This fire is the will of heaven come to earth, the very definition of the Kingdom of God. "Your kingdom come. Your will be done, on earth as it is in heaven" (Matthew 6:10).

Our prayers in this day as we live in a strategic interval in salvation history are vital. During this Revelation 8:2–5 interval, the power of the prophetic will be renewed and purified because this intercession must be informed prophetically in order for it to reflect the heart of God.

Bringing It Home

Lest the outpouring of the Kingdom of God in response to prayer become too ethereal a concept and we become so spiritual that we can no longer be practical, let me say that none of it matters if we cannot bring it home. In personal testimony, here is how basic it gets. Apply this to your own life and relationships.

I cry, "Change me, O God! Make me like You!" but I am a slob by nature. Not that my personal hygiene suffers. I simply fail to see the point in making a bed that I will get back into tonight when no one will ever see it made. Or, why wash the dishes before the sink is full? Why empty the dishwasher when I can leave the dishes in there where they will only get cleaner with each cycle? Why put my dirty clothes in the hamper every day when I can do it once a week? Are they not just as well preserved on the floor by the bed as in the laundry room?

If I lived alone, all of this would be irrelevant, but I married an obsessive-compulsive woman where "clean" is concerned. She associates love and security with clean and tidy. If I get up from the table to go to the bathroom during dinner, I have to announce that I will return in a moment because in the absence of that announcement, my plate will be in the dishwasher before I get back. She exclaims that the house is filthy, goes into an extended cleaning frenzy and then wants to know if I notice. Because her dirty is most people's spotless, I genuinely cannot tell the difference and so I say, "Yes dear, I see. The house looks great!"

What does the Kingdom of God, the will of heaven come to earth, strategic prayer in a strategic time, have to do with that? Acceleration! Even the smallest imperfections and compromises will come under God's magnifying glass and cost us dearly in the strategic days before us. The time is long past for some of us to stop thinking about why our needs are not being met at home and to begin thinking about the Kingdom of God where we live. Selflessness! Intensification of love! The servant heart! Heart of the Father! Fail in these things and our prayers for the realization of the Kingdom of God on earth will mean very little.

At home the Kingdom is grace, love, the servant heart and laying my life down for my wife. It took nearly thirty years for me to get it, but today I pick up my clothes and I put my own dishes in the dishwasher on my own—if I can beat her to it—because that is service, and that is love. I finally grew up, and it matters.

Sometimes the Kingdom means giving my vacation days to a staff member who has used up all of hers or his in an extended illness so that they will not suffer financial hardship. Maybe you have a boss who practices management by intimidation. The Kingdom of God, heaven's will come to earth, means honoring, forgiving, praying for, blessing and doing the best job you can, no matter what.

It means the guy who cut me off on the freeway and nearly caused an accident is not an idiot who has earned my curses, but a desperate sinner whom God loves. I probably did not even see his face, but in the Kingdom of God, the will of heaven come to earth, I must bless and I must sow blessing, even when no one sees or hears.

Above all, as we have been gifted with the mind and Spirit of Christ, it means that we have been empowered to do these things. Kingdom fire cast into the earth compels us to do these things. The intensity of our prayers during this Revelation 8:2–5 interval opens doors to the kind of outpouring that changes our character inwardly and results in power outwardly. We change in the mundane, in the privacy of our homes, and therefore cause change in the wider world. The Kingdom of God has come among us and will manifest with ever-increasing power for every level of life as we devote ourselves to prayer with the heart of the Father leading us.

Affecting the World

Prayer for the manifestation of the Kingdom means that President Obama is not the Antichrist as some misguided Christians would have us believe, but just a man who needs the touch of God, very much perhaps like those Roman emperors who committed ungodly acts in the days of the apostle

John. In fact, I believe prophetically that if the saints will pray and not condemn as we have so often done, the president will experience a dramatic encounter with the living God while in office that will transform his faith and his life. Scripture calls us to pray "for kings and all who are in authority, so that we may lead a tranquil and quiet life in all godliness and dignity" (1 Timothy 2:2).

Absolutely conditional, this prophetic word concerning the president depends on our obedience to the heart of the Father for its fulfillment. Do it, and wonderful things may come to pass. Do it not, and nothing will happen at all. At the end of the first three centuries, the Church conquered the Roman Empire through love and prayer magnified by the angels of heaven as they lived the Kingdom of God on a daily basis. Nothing has changed. God's way stands the test of time.

Much prophecy takes the form of "if-then." *If* we will adjust our attitude, *then* God will restore our public and societal influence and sovereignly place us in positions of influence in a time of trouble just as He did Joseph with Pharaoh and Daniel with Nebuchadnezzar. Fail in this and we will continue to be perceived as a growing societal threat, a negative force, our voice and influence marginalized.

Conclusion

The fire of the altar cast into the earth begins here and here it applies. It must penetrate the small things in our lives before we will have credibility in the big things. The trumpet will sound sometime soon and judgment will fall as this interval in time comes to a close. Jesus must soon return. We live in the time of Revelation 8:2–5, a season like no other in my lifetime or yours. Pray. Pray for the Kingdom to come, and know that heaven itself empowers it. Plumb the depths of what this means and implies at every level of life. Take the Kingdom to the world, but take it home too.

Know that in this day, the angels in heaven amplify our prayers and that our prayers ascend to heaven as a pleasing aroma to our God. Expect fire, holy fire, the very presence of God, to fall in response to those prayers in a way and with an intensity we have never known.

Expect breakthroughs like we have never seen breakthroughs before. Expect people to come to know Jesus. Expect miracles. Expect healings to increase. Expect lives to change and marriages to be restored. Expect addictions to be broken. Expect an increase in power to flow through us. Expect things that once seemed difficult, things that existed at one time only in promise, to become reality much more easily than we ever dreamed.

What was work and labor will become joy. Doors that were closed will open. Blockages that kept you from flowing in love or prevented you from receiving or ministering healing, or that anchored you in an old way, or kept you from advancing, or muted your witness in the world, will fall before you because God will cast fire into the earth before the day of judgment comes. Expect changes.

We live in the interlude before the trumpets blow, a season for the most intense prayer of our lives, a season for glory and opportunity. Time to wake up and pray! God is moving both in the earth and in the heavens and we must move with Him. The cloud of glory goes before us and we must follow.

11

THE CLOUD OF GLORY HAS MOVED

Now Moses used to take the tent and pitch it outside the camp, a good distance from the camp, and he called it the tent of meeting. And everyone who sought the LORD would go out to the tent of meeting which was outside the camp. And it came about, whenever Moses went out to the tent, that all the people would arise and stand, each at the entrance of his tent, and gaze after Moses until he entered the tent. Whenever Moses entered the tent, the pillar of cloud would descend and stand at the entrance of the tent; and the LORD would speak with Moses. When all the people saw the pillar of cloud standing at the entrance of the tent, all the people would arise and worship, each at the entrance of his tent.

Exodus 33:7–10

In Moses' day, the cloud of glory descended as the visible evidence or sense of the presence of God. We can define glory as the radiant and sometimes visible goodness of God flowing from His presence that we feel and occasionally see.

Glory and the presence of God form a package to be experienced simultaneously as the tangible sense of His love and peace, the heat you feel or the electricity that courses through your body when someone prays for you. You know, then, that you have been touched by something different and more wonderful than anything you have ever known.

At my church when the glory has fallen we have heard—and recorded—audible angel song. From time to time angelic instruments have played along with the worship band. These manifestations have been objectively measurable, much as was the cloud of glory in Moses' day. As when Israel traveled through the wilderness, the glory results in miracles of deliverance, healing and mercy. Seventy percent of my congregation say they have experienced a significant physical healing at our church. The same is true wherever the cloud descends.

Priorities

When God shows Himself, those who love Him present themselves, figuratively speaking, at the doors of their tents and stand to honor Him with their full attention. In recent days the cloud has appeared in our midst in many forms as God has manifested Himself with increasing demonstrations of His love and power. We *must* come to the doors of our homes, our lives, to stand at attention and to focus on the Presence and worship.

No matter what has been going on in your home, your family or your life, you must set it behind you. Nothing can be allowed to take precedence over a focus on the presence of God. His presence must overshadow any trouble or problem that might be lodged in the tent of your life. The New Testament knows this as "seek first His kingdom and His righteousness" with the promise that all these other concerns will be taken care of (Matthew 6:33).

Motion

In accord with a singular focus on the appearance of the cloud of glory, when the cloud moved, the people of Israel packed their things and moved with it. From Exodus 13:21–22 onward, Moses led hundreds of thousands of Israelites out of slavery in Egypt and through the wilderness as God guided them:

> The Lord was going before them in a pillar of cloud by day to lead them on the way, and in a pillar of fire by night to give them light, that they might travel by day and by night. He did not take away the pillar of cloud by day, nor the pillar of fire by night, from before the people.

The cloud moved "that they might travel." This held true throughout forty years of wandering until the people entered the Promised Land. God in His goodness takes His people somewhere, ever moving them toward a goal and a promise. When the glory cloud—the presence of God—moves, God's people follow.

In Jesus the same holds true as He constantly moves us toward a goal in glory and expects us to follow. No one can enter into the place of promise if they will not move when the cloud of glory moves.

Where It Leads

I was seven years old in 1958 when my parents fell headlong into the charismatic renewal, led their church into it and then became international leaders in the movement. As a result, as previously noted, I have seen many movements and their emphases come and go as the cloud of glory led the Body of Christ through various phases of preparation for the times in which we now live. Painstakingly, the stage has been set for the greatest move of the Spirit since Pentecost. We have seen renewal, physical healing, inner healing, prophetic ministry, signs and wonders and more. God intended these things to prepare us for Kingdom glory and ministry. Along the way we have cried out for the fullness of revival, but strange as it may sound, God has more in store for us than mere revival.

Previous movements eventually devolved into self-focus and nearly ground to a halt, even if the forms and the noise of those movements continued in styles and practices long after the glory faded. Inevitably, self-focus kills. This time, however, things can be different. The cloud of glory has moved into an emphasis on the Kingdom of God—the government of God come to earth—infused with His nature and character. It manifests in Spirit-empowered acts of mercy and miracles, which cannot and must not be co-opted into an emphasis on self. We enter the Kingdom in the selflessness of the character of Jesus or we enter not at all. Each individual must determine to live beyond himself or herself for the sake of the Lord and others or be left behind. There can be no in-between.

In the Kingdom of God we live for a purpose greater than ourselves to affect and change the world around us by ministering the powers of heaven and the law of love come to earth. Until now too many of us have been much too absorbed in receiving experiences, being healed and getting personally blessed. Now the cloud of glory has moved and the anointing has shifted. No longer does it linger over the concern for personal growth, healing and blessing. God will continue to heal us, bless us and cause us to grow as individuals, but this can no longer be the focus. The anointing has shifted.

We may want to camp on some great moment of the Lord's outpouring, but the time has come to pack up our households and all we have. We must put every issue of life behind us—blessings, problems, loves, hates, fears, joys and hurts—and move.

Your Personal Benefit

If you will focus your life and household on following the cloud into this shift of emphasis, serving the Kingdom of God and orienting everything that you do and everything that you are toward that goal, you will be absorbed in a selfless purpose that will order and heal your home and your life. More than this, it will revolutionize your church and make it a force for change. Relationships with a purpose beyond themselves survive and thrive as they are given away. Those relationships that exist for their own sake die. "For whoever wishes to save his life will lose it; but whoever loses his life for My sake will find it" (Matthew 16:25).

Provided you make the right choices, as the world enters the coming time of severe crisis you will be filled up with the joy of bearing fruit for a purpose greater than yourself. Depression and fear will be canceled out. Families will heal and churches will unite around the one purpose that transcends selfish concerns. Addictions will be conquered because you will be obsessed with helping others out of their addictions and you will be walking in the power of the Kingdom as you do it.

Five years to prepare gives us time to orient our lives, our attitudes and our character around the cloud of glory as it draws us into the Kingdom of God to touch the world around us with power. As sin bears its inevitable destructive fruit, desperate people will seek answers in the supernatural and in the Father's love and we must be ready to provide them. We have been granted a period of preparation in which to work free of the culture of self by the power of the Holy Spirit so we can effectively follow the cloud of glory.

From Slavery to Freedom

When the cloud moved, God led Israel from what had become comfortable slavery in Egypt into an uncomfortable freedom.

In slavery they knew where they would sleep at night and where the next meal would come from. By contrast, in freedom nothing was certain. Likewise, today God keeps us in motion, moving us forward out of the comfort zone, awakening us from spiritual slumber, in order to bless us to participate in His Kingdom.

If we will not move and if we fail to grow, we will die. In this crucial time of preparation and in the days beyond it, God has reserved a glorious destiny for each of us to rise into. The world may disintegrate around us, but we Kingdom believers will find ourselves walking in more light and power than we ever imagined we could, free of fear, expecting and ministering great things of God.

We have been born for this and many of us have experienced a lifetime of preparation for it. When trouble rises in the world, the power of God in love rises to overcome. In the midst of crisis, just as He displayed His greatness through deliverance for the people of Israel, God wants to show off His sons and daughters to a desperate world as He pours out His power through them and for them.

When the glory descends on His people and the world sees Him doing great and miraculous things for them and through them, God gets a reputation. No good testimony could come from a people camped out on the shore of the Red Sea waiting to be annihilated. The spectacle of a people moving forward through the sea made a declaration to the nations. The glory of God therefore moves us through crisis on all sides in the midst of perceived risk and fear toward a destination and a destiny, but in the risk lies blessing for us and a reputation for God. It is not easy and it is not comfortable but it is glorious.

The Problem with Stagnation

As a law of nature, if we remain in one place long enough we stink it up through stagnation that turns even good things bad.

Too many of us have lost the renewal we once knew because we chose to camp out in an old place after the cloud of glory had moved on. Consequently, revival died and we have wondered where it went ever since.

I planted a church in the Coeur d'Alene, Idaho, area in 1980 and pastored it for eleven years, several years beyond the point at which the glory cloud had moved. By the time I finally left, I had sunk deep into burnout and the church had suffered a number of disasters and setbacks that had sucked the life from it. I stayed too long, having failed to move on because of fear of loss—my family's ministry at Elijah House, the church itself, our home, my parents and five siblings. As a result, things got smelly. I was miserable, but no longer.

Beth and I have been married since 1972 and the years have been good to us. From the beginning we chose to focus our marriage on the Kingdom of God and on following the cloud of glory. That focus and purpose beyond ourselves has kept us in love and at peace all these years. Life lines up behind it. From time to time, we moved late when the cloud moved on, as when we stayed too long in Idaho, and then had to suffer the resulting mess, but we have always followed in the end. This has kept us alive and in love.

In this season of preparation we must come to the door of our tents, leaving behind the messes inside, and focus on the cloud, the ever-moving presence of God. "Seek first His kingdom . . . and all these things will be added to you" (Matthew 6:33), and, "Everyone who has left houses or brothers or sisters or father or mother or children or farms for My name's sake, will receive many times as much, and will inherit eternal life" (Matthew 19:29).

In this season ahead of us, if you remain focused on self, meeting personal needs, wallowing in personal fears, gnawing on bitterness over the failures of people around you, protecting yourself against real and imagined hurt, you will stink up your life and your church and remain bankrupt. Move with the cloud and you will have the time of your life ministering the life-changing power of the Kingdom of God in signs, wonders and miracles of healing. These will become crucially important in the dark days to come.

The Principle of Motion

God built the universe on the principle of motion. This book you hold in your hand is no solid object, but rather energy contained in atoms like little solar systems, each with a nucleus and tiny electron particles made of energy spinning around the nucleus. The earth spins on its axis as it orbits the sun. The solar system orbits the galaxy. Motion. Always motion. The air we breathe moves. The water in the sea flows with the Gulf Stream. Because movement energizes and oxygenates, when motion stops, everything dies.

I once shut off the pumps that aerate my very large fish tank. Within a half a day I found my fish gasping for oxygen at the surface of the water. Without motion, water cannot absorb oxygen. Life itself is like that. Motion cleanses and keeps us healthy.

The presence of God is about life, and life is growth and motion. How can God be glorified if we receive salvation but continue in dysfunction and sin? God makes Himself look good by making us look good. Change—movement—is therefore the essence of the Kingdom of God. Change frightens us, but if we fail to move with it, we die. In the days to come, change will come ever more quickly as history rushes toward its climax in the Lord's return. We live in a season of acceleration, remember?

Strive to recognize motion and change during this period of preparation for the difficult times to come. At so many levels heaven calls us into the Kingdom of God so that we might minister to a world about to experience a level of need unprecedented in our lifetimes.

Now and in the days to come God calls us to move in levels of power we have never yet experienced and to do it in the midst of times of difficulty in the material world. As we find ourselves forced to depend on Him for daily sustenance in ways we never did before—shades of "manna"—we will be called upon to exercise authority in ministry to others in ways we never conceived of for ourselves.

This has already begun. Things we once allowed leadership to do for us—prophetic ministry, healing, signs and wonders—are now up to the ordinary believer as God retires and even destroys the star system under which we have operated for so very long. A period of preparation lies before us—five literal or figurative years of grace—in which to learn, in which to move with the cloud of glory carrying us beyond ourselves and into the Kingdom of God whose law is the selflessness of the cross and the power of the resurrection.

Take Me Back to Egypt

The deepening crises to come will affect us materially in the same way as these crises will affect those in the world. As this season for preparation comes to a close and difficult times intensify, the tendency will be to romanticize past seasons of life, forgetting the dissatisfaction and even the misery we felt there. The difference between us and the world, however, will lie in the One we have with us and in the joy that sustains us as we walk into the future in Kingdom love, Kingdom power and Kingdom authority.

If, however, we have camped out at an earlier stage along the way, we will be crying, "Take me back to Egypt. I was comfortable there. I'm sorry I moved."

The cloud, the presence of God, takes us to unfamiliar places that we are unprepared to face unless we have decided to come out to the door of our tents with our backs to the past and our self-centered problems in order to focus on the glory, pack up everything and move with Him. We either trust Him or we go back to slavery. In the coming days this choice will become more sharply focused.

"The LORD said to Moses, 'How long will this people spurn Me? And how long will they not believe in Me, despite all the signs which I have performed in their midst?'" (Numbers 14:11). Perhaps you have seen the wonders, the demonstration of power and the healings. Maybe God has provided for you over and over again in the midst of uncertainty. You have seen your own life change and yet when that army approaches, that threatening situation, force of opposition or situation that appears to be impossible, fear gets a grip on you and leads you into unbelief. Even though the cloud has moved, you have difficulty moving with it.

How many of us fear to step across boundaries to grow into something greater or to minister the power of God to people who do not yet know Jesus? God has provided a passage through your Red Sea but you fear those walls of water. You can have a tremendous personal encounter with God, only to lose it because God moved and fear or unbelief kept you anchored in an old place. God says to Israel, "Why have you spurned Me?" When we refuse to obey Him or to move forward with Him in response to the word His prophet speaks, then we have spurned and rejected God.

Neither the *emotion* of fear nor the *feeling* of unbelief make up rejection of God. *Acting* on that fear and *acting* in unbelief constitute unbelief. In the coming years we will experience the same pressures as the rest of the world, but we must respond in faith and authority, not in acts of unbelief.

Summary

Many of us now have entered a time when we must move from the focus on personal healing and restoration—the emphasis for the last forty years—into the selflessness of the Kingdom of God. The cloud of glory has gone before us into the age of the Kingdom of God in which every individual believer, gifted to minister the power of God to a world desperately in need of salvation, boldly crosses boundaries to demonstrate the power of that Kingdom to a lost world. The cloud has moved and destiny is at our doorstep, but if we fail to pack up everything and move with it, we stink up our house and die.

God has never asked me if I felt ready to follow or obey Him. He never asked my permission when He wanted me to move into something new, to take a risk, to step into a new ministry or to take on a new responsibility. He simply went before me and expected me to follow. He did not ask what was happening in my life or how I felt about it. He just moved.

I do not really know how much or how little time we have to prepare. Five years can be figurative for an indeterminate period of grace or it can be a literal five years that began in May 2010. I suspect that however long a time it may be, it can be extended by prayer. I do know that the cloud of glory has already moved and that the anointing has shifted. When you hear the prophetic word to move forward, therefore, do it and do it now. It will lead you to your blessing and to His glory and honor. Otherwise you may find yourself among those who fall away.

12

THE GREAT APOSTASY

At that time many will fall away and will betray one another and hate one another. Many false prophets will arise and will mislead many.

Matthew 24:10–11

Now we request you, brethren, with regard to the coming of our Lord Jesus Christ and our gathering together to Him, that you not be quickly shaken from your composure or be disturbed either by a spirit or a message or a letter as if from us, to the effect that the day of the Lord has come. Let no one in any way deceive you, for it will not come unless the apostasy comes first.

2 Thessalonians 2:1–3

I find myself appalled concerning a trend I have seen developing in the Body of Christ for several years now. This trend propels us toward a crisis in the charismatic Christian world that may well derail and destroy a great many followers before they can join the coming move of the Spirit into the reality of the Kingdom of God. A set of cracks has already opened up in renewal circles that will quietly widen into division over the course of the five to ten years to come. The center of the chasm consists of conflict over the gradual erosion of central Christian doctrines, acceptance of extra-biblical revelation as fact and the proliferation of aberrant ministry practices. To a lesser degree it involves questions involving sin in leadership, acceptance of it and conditions of restoration for fallen leaders.

I believe much of this to be part of the Great Apostasy taking root in places we never expected. In ways few concerned revival leaders have yet spoken of openly, a line is being drawn in the sand by those who remain committed to solid grounding in our historic biblical faith. I believe a remnant will stand and remain steadfast—the revealed sons and daughters of God—but significant damage will be done before the dust settles.

Much of the impetus to depart from the plumb line of solid Christian doctrine and from responsible and accurate interpretation of the Scriptures stems from the growing quest to become supernatural. The consequent search for more and deeper revelation has led to dangerous compromises of clear scriptural teaching. Behind it all stands both a desire to access more power and a serious lack of real faith in the sufficiency and potency of the cross and the resurrection.

Paul wrote, "For I am not ashamed of the gospel, for it is the power of God for salvation to everyone who believes, to the Jew first and also to the Greek" (Romans 1:16). One could wonder to what degree many of us really still believe this, or did we forget the exhortation in Hebrews 13:9: "Do not be carried away by varied and strange teachings; for it is good for the heart to be strengthened by grace, not by foods, through which those who were so occupied were not benefited."

The weirdness flowing from key leaders in various places is leading many followers into what can only be called heresy. This is not the place for an extended exercise in apologetics. I will neither fully explain nor comprehensively debate the tenets of these examples of aberrant doctrine and practice. I will simply name some representative examples, summarize them and briefly point out the more obvious fallacies.

Out of respect and consideration for those involved I choose not to name names. Many of these people have had a huge positive impact on the Body of Christ in spite of some areas of error in their teaching. I honor this, but in the same way that Paul pointed out the dangers inherent in the teachings of the Judaizers and confronted Peter's compromise when he refused to eat with Gentiles, I must point out some false doctrines, aberrant practices and looming dangers. I do this knowing that the trend will continue, despite the warnings and pleadings of those of us who raise the alarm. The Great Apostasy has begun, and I am not speaking figuratively.

Heresy

Here are some heretical teachings in the Church today.

Open Theism

Some prominent teachers in the renewal movement now espouse "open theism," which at its root asserts that God does not know the future, the end from the beginning. It then builds on that premise to diminish the revelation of the omniscience and absolute power of our God that Scripture so clearly articulates. Some protest that this is God's own self-limitation, not an actual one. In either case, if God does not know the end from the beginning and if He has not decreed the course of history, remaining in control of it, then every prophecy of the Old and New Testaments is invalid, as are most forms of modern prophetic ministry.

Open theists often protest that God cannot have both fore-knowledge and sovereignty without interfering with human freedom of choice, as if the two were mutually exclusive ideas that must cancel one another out or force a choice for one or the other. False! Both the Jews and Pontius Pilate made free human choices to crucify Jesus and yet the Scripture clearly states that Jesus accomplished the cross by the predetermined plan and foreknowledge of God. If the open theists have it right, then Jesus could not have been delivered up by the predetermined plan and foreknowledge of God as Scripture so clearly teaches (see Acts 2:23).

As evidence for their position, some open theists point to passages that say that God changed His mind, and yet in other places God says that He is not a man that He should change His mind (see Numbers 23:19; 1 Samuel 15:29). Why not see such statements as God graciously engaging Moses and others in the process for the sake of relationship, even while knowing the outcome He had predetermined? The Hebrew mind had no problem balancing paradoxes, of which there are many in Scripture. Why should we?

In the opening chapters of Ephesians Paul wrote that He chose us before the foundation of the world for good works that God prepared beforehand that we should walk in them (see 2:10). Predetermination in no way negates or interferes with the freedom of human choice. Yes, this presents us with paradoxes and mysteries, but is that not the nature of God? Open theism is nothing more than the attempt of modern Western minds, steeped in Western philosophy, to reduce the infinite to the level of the finite and to shrink God to the level of our own ability to understand.

No Need to Repent

Another teaching gaining ground among us poses the idea that once we have come to Jesus we need never again repent because we have been fully sanctified and are no longer sinners. Yes, we have been fully forgiven for all our sin, past, present and future. True, we have been fully sanctified and have become the righteousness of God. Absolutely, we have been made completely holy by the finished work of the cross. This does not, however, mean that we now behave perfectly at all times or that our character has now been completely transformed to reflect that of Jesus, nor does it mean that we never wander from the path or that we never cause wounding to anyone.

If we need never repent again then why would Paul speak to the Christians in Corinth of the godly sorrow that produces a repentance without regret (see 2 Corinthians 7:10)? In that passage he spoke to believers concerning the quality of sorrow they needed to experience concerning the sin they were committing. Did God not call believers to repent who were members of the churches addressed in the book of Revelation?

Repentance means that when I have done wrong, I must make a 180-degree turn to rectify the error. I am empowered to do this, why? Because I have already been forgiven and made holy, because I wish to work out the salvation I have already received (see Philippians 2:12), and because I must pursue the sanctification without which I cannot see or experience God (see Hebrews 12:14). Some of us need to do a thorough study of New Testament exhortations to repent.

Universalism

Is God so kind that He could never consign anyone to hell? Does the scriptural assertion that God is not willing that any should perish mean that no one does and that all go to heaven? Universalism teaches that no one goes to hell and that all are saved. In some cases it insists that hell does not even exist.

If all are saved regardless of their relationship to Jesus, then Jesus lied when He said that He alone is the way, the truth and the life (see John 14:6). When the Philippian jailer asked Paul and Silas, "'Sirs, what must I do to be saved?' They said, 'Believe in the Lord Jesus, and you will be saved, you and your household'" (Acts 16:30–31). Apart from such faith, there could be no salvation. Romans 5:9 and the verses following clearly state the requirement of reconciliation with God and make it clear that this can only happen through the mediation of Jesus.

On the existence of hell Scripture speaks just as clearly. If hell does not exist, then from what have we been saved and for what did Jesus die? The apostle James believed in hell (see James 3:6). So did Peter (see 2 Peter 2:4). Paul says of those who do not know God, "These will pay the penalty of eternal destruction, away from the presence of the Lord and from the glory of His power" (2 Thessalonians 1:9).

Heaven holds no suffering, no tears, no evil, no hate. God's paradise consists of eternal bliss, but to hear some people talk you would think that in heaven we forever sit around passively smoking legalized marijuana, eating peyote buttons for Communion bread and drinking Jack Daniels for the wine, eternally stoned.

Heaven, however, is not a place of passive bliss. In heaven we engage in active relationships of love and live in constant perfected worship offered up by those who have been made perfect by the transforming power of God. If you were evil here and nothing has happened to change you, you will be evil in the afterlife. If you were unforgiving here and you have not set a course to be conformed to the image of Jesus (see Romans 8:29), you will be unforgiving there. If you pursued a selfish lifestyle here you will be selfish there, unless the change began on earth in your passionate love for God and in your oneness with Jesus who made you holy.

I am not speaking of achieving perfection this side of the resurrection. I speak rather of the course you have set for your life and whether your heart is truly repentant. Or will you appear before the throne of heaven and protest that your perception of reality is right and His is wrong? Are you so sure of yourself?

The point: If God were to allow into heaven unrepentant people who hate—the rebellious ones, the disobedient ones, the unchanged abusers of this world, or at the extreme end, the Adolf Hitlers and the Osama bin Ladens—unchanged and unrepentant, then it would no longer be heaven, would it? They would make heaven into the hell they created on this earth. A place with no tears and no torment would become a place of suffering and we would be right back where we started. Is God too nice, too loving to consign anyone to hell? The truth is that God is too nice and too loving *not* to consign some to hell, and none of us is as good as we want to fool ourselves into believing.

No matter how good I have been in this life, if I have ever lied, then I am not a good person. I am a liar. No matter how righteously I have lived, even if I only once sank into pornography, then I am not a good person but rather an adulterer. A thief goes to jail as the penalty for one theft. No matter how well he lived his life before, one crime brings the penalty. All have sinned (see Romans 3:23). All deserve the penalty. Jesus alone suffered the sentence we deserved, but we must receive Him by faith in order to appropriate the gift. Failure to do so results in there being no sacrifice for sin, but only the certainty of judgment (see Hebrews 10:26–27). Hell is real. We need a Savior.

If sinners apart from Christ are not in heaven, then where are they? They are cut off from the presence of God because the unholy cannot exist in the presence of the holy. Those who believe have been made holy by the sacrifice Jesus offered on the cross and by our willingness to become one with Him in all that He is. The very existence of a heaven with God therefore requires that there be a hell without Him or else heaven ceases to be heaven.

Cheap Grace

Related to the various forms of universalism is an epidemic of cheap grace that has infected and sickened the Western church. The second and third chapters of Revelation include the letters to the seven churches of Asia. The letter to Ephesus says that God hates the deeds of the Nicolaitans (see 2:6). The Nicolaitans taught cheap grace, that the grace of God somehow allows us to live in any manner of sin we choose because God forgives. The exhortation to Pergamum condemns the church in that city for tolerating the teaching of Balaam "who kept teaching Balak to put a stumbling block before the sons of Israel, to eat things sacrificed to idols and to commit acts of immorality" (2:14). In 2:21, the Lord indicts Thyatira for tolerating Jezebel, who led the people to commit acts of immorality, and He pronounces death and pestilence on her and her followers if they will not repent.

Too many churches no longer stand firmly for morality and a higher standard. Seeking numbers, they set the bar lower than God's commandments and ordinances in order to make it easier to fill the seats. I hope the church I pastor grows exponentially, but God did not call us to build large churches and expand our numbers. He called us to make disciples. I choose to trust God that the making of disciples will feed the growth of the church and increase the numbers of those being genuinely saved. We have, however, compromised God's principles to a greater degree than many of us have been willing to admit and then we wonder why the culture around us has not been affected by the power entrusted to us by Almighty God.

In short, too many prominent Christian leaders have become heretics leading the masses away from the revelation of truth received once for all in the infallible Word of God. In doing so, they cease to be genuinely Christian. The Great Apostasy has begun and it will bring about the downfall of prominent ministries and mega-churches in years to come. Already we have seen it begin. We will see an acceleration of this as the revelation of the powerlessness of such teaching unfolds and spreads like wildfire. The outcome is certain. It will happen.

From the Heretical to the Silly

The problem stretches from the heretical to the silly. On a ministry trip to New Zealand I learned of one prominent leader who teaches that we can unleash our spirituality by taking monoatomic gold pills. Why? Because Adam was made of monoatomic gold. What? Where is the scriptural or archeological evidence for this nonsense? But how wonderful! Now we can avoid the need to die with Christ. We no longer need to be selfless and Christlike! All we have to do is take a pill! Having looked up monoatomic gold on YouTube, I find it to be expensive stuff to purchase, which could explain the motivation for the teaching.

Another teacher here in the United States tells audiences that God did not part the Red Sea, Moses did! He intends to communicate the power and authority God has given to us as believers, but minimizes both the Source of that power and the Scripture itself when it says, "*the* LORD swept the sea back by a strong east wind all night" (Exodus 14:21, emphasis mine). What about Acts 3 where Peter protests to the lame beggar that he has nothing to give him but Jesus? Where is our discernment?

From another source I have heard it taught that it would be all right to pierce the ear in the lobe, but not at the top because the top is the ear gate and you might hinder your ability to hear God. Where is there any real foundation for this in God's Word? I know what you are thinking. This seems a minor issue, but it speaks to the unbiblical silliness and foolish assumptions that seem to be multiplying in the charismatic world.

I am aware of one Christian leader who has devised a method of Christian divination in the form of astrology, claiming that in doing so he has redeemed something for Christian use that the enemy stole. What happened to the biblical injunction against engaging in this kind of activity and the penalties for doing it (see Deuteronomy 18:10–12; Isaiah 47:12–14)?

This merely scratches the surface with a few representative examples. Where do we find the justification for any of this when held up to the light of solid exegesis of God's Word? And if exegesis is a foreign word, take some time to look it up and learn to understand how to read the Bible accurately for what it actually says. It is long since time for us to stop interpreting the Scriptures through the filter of our personal revelations and personal experiences and learn to interpret our personal revelations and personal experiences by the Bible.

Prophetically Speaking

Some time ago my friend Fred Wright (founding coordinator of Partners in Harvest) and I were discussing the state of the prophetic movement and the plethora of bad prophecy flowing from leading prophetic voices. He said, "If something isn't done soon, the prophetic movement is over in five years." He was right. In more than just prophetic ministry we have been focused on being supernatural and getting the next "word" at the expense of intimacy with the One for whom we have been called to speak.

Too often, we have failed to separate our own emotions from the true prophetic word flowing from the heart of God. As a result we end up prophesying words from our own imaginations and desires. Many have been doing what Jeremiah cried out against in Jeremiah 23:30, "Therefore behold, I am against the prophets . . . who steal My words from each other." It works like this: We hear prophecies from one another that excite our emotions in both positive and negative ways. Then in our flesh we build on what has excited us, failing to differentiate between personal feelings and the voice of God, until the words we speak go well beyond the truth of God's heart. Skewed and extreme statements result that either raise false expectations of great things or feed excessive fear and dread. Not the truth!

Please know that I am a dyed-in-the-wool "River" person. I cherish the move of the Spirit. I love it when God makes a sovereign "mess" of a meeting and people fall, laugh, cry and shake. People receive miraculous healing in my church on a regular basis. I love good prophetic ministry. As I mentioned earlier, we have heard audible angel song in some of our meetings and actually caught it on a recording. I am by no means a revival critic, but I have been given a prophetic voice and I must use it to sound the alarm when God calls me to do so.

These aberrations I have called attention to represent a mere sampling of the utter nonsense growing in renewal circles these days and being passed off as revelation by a number of key leaders and prophetic voices. Those who have attempted to stand against this pollution of the stream have sometimes been vilified, accused of creating division and of squelching the Spirit. They would be in good company where creating division is concerned. Jeremiah! Micaiah! Paul! Jesus Himself!

For my part, I state prophetically that the great end time apostasy prophesied in Scripture (see Matthew 24:10; 2 Thessalonians 2:3) has begun, but it has taken root in unexpected places where misguided leaders and teachers present personal revelation as fact and where these twist the Scriptures to make them appear to support propositions based on grains of truth driven to extremes that render them false. Heresies and spiritual silliness result.

Time to Refocus

If you focus on being supernatural you will end up in shipwreck, but if you focus on being intimate with the Father you will end up being supernatural. Does that not sound like Jesus? Or might it be more true that we need to focus not on being prophetic as much as being sons and daughters of God? In too many places our hunger has shifted from longing to be one with Jesus—and with our Father through Him—to a focus on seeking supernatural experiences. Having fallen into a form of idolatry, we then long for the effect rather than real relationship with the Cause. Or we search for the next great spiritual revelation and forget that the most foundational revelation of all is the Father's heart of love, the gift of His Son to die in our place and the invitation given us to grow up to be like Him in every aspect of our character, "conformed to the image of His Son" (Romans 8:29).

This calls for a renewed emphasis on the cross where we die with Christ, the blood that cleanses us from sin and the resurrection that gives us new life. Paul said—and with good reason—"For I determined to know nothing among you except Jesus Christ, and Him crucified" (1 Corinthians 2:2). In addition to that, did we forget that the word *canon* with reference to the Scriptures means the "fence" beyond which we cannot go, that we can neither add to nor detract from? In too many places the focus has shifted and we are about to find ourselves impaled on hidden reefs of destruction.

I realize that this is not the kind of word that produces invitations to speak at big conferences and that it puts me on the outs with certain other leaders in renewal circles. I cannot say that I care nothing for that, but I can say that I will be true to the quest to know my Father's heart and that I will govern my revelations of Him and from Him by the plumb line of Scripture delivered once for all. I will issue the warning that we are heading increasingly down a very dangerous path. I pray for a revelation of the heart of the Father to restore us to ourselves before it is too late.

13

THE SAMSON GENERATION

And the Prophetic Significance of the Fortieth Anniversary of the Woodstock Festival

While making specific reference to the Jewish people, the apostle Paul set forth the general principle that "the gifts and the calling of God are irrevocable" (Romans 11:29). When, therefore, God calls a people or a generation and then bestows gifts upon them to carry out the calling, this cannot be revoked, nor can those so called ever be released. God does not change His mind.

Judges 16 tells of a period in Israel's history when the nation repeatedly suffered devastating attacks at the hands of the Philistines. With no central government and no standing army, the better armed, better organized Philistines raided and plundered the people almost at will. In response, God raised up judges whose gifts and callings were irrevocable to lead the people in their own defense.

Because our heavenly Father seems to revel in patterns, some predictions of the future reflect past events. "That which has been is that which will be, and that which has been done is that which will be done. So there is nothing new under the sun" (Ecclesiastes 1:9). I draw the following parallels from the situation in which Israel found itself during the period of the judges. This prediction of the future therefore reflects the patterns of the past and builds upon the events of the present.

Samson

Among the judges God appointed to deliver Israel so long ago came Samson, born a Nazirite, dedicated to God from birth. Gifted with incredible skill in battle and superhuman strength to back it up, he became a terror to Israel's enemies. It all flowed from the length of his hair, the mark of his calling and identity.

If captured and bound, he broke the ropes. With nothing but the jawbone from a dead donkey he once single-handedly killed a thousand Philistines. Brute strength enabled him to pull up the gates of cities by the posts. God blessed him with an irrevocable calling and with the gifting to carry it out.

Enter Delilah. Through Delilah, Samson allowed himself to be seduced by the lusts of the flesh. One of the most masterful testosterone manipulations in recorded history followed as Delilah worked him with love and lust until he revealed to her the secret of his strength.

> She made him sleep on her knees, and called for a man and had him shave off the seven locks of his hair. Then she began to afflict him, and his strength left him. . . . Then the Philistines seized him and gouged out his eyes; and they brought him down to

Gaza and bound him with bronze chains, and he was a grinder in the prison.

Judges 16:19, 21

The Samson Paradigm

Samson's life forms a paradigm for the post–World War II generation. The first lesson of that life can be expressed in a simple principle: When you abandon the calling and lay down the gifting God bestowed on you, you become blind and the enemy of your soul binds you in chains of futility and hopelessness. You find yourself imprisoned in a dark world of self, wandering in circles like Samson at the grinding wheel, void of purpose. You no longer see or perceive God as you once did, and life loses its light and joy. As the grinding wheel weighs heavily on your spirit, depression sets in. This was Samson, and this describes the life of every servant of God or generation of people who abandon the calling of God and His gifts in favor of some lesser pursuit.

Remember, however, that God does not change His mind. Both the gifts and the calling remain, held in trust, irrevocable, against the day of His return. He will neither cancel the contract nor nullify the covenant. Samson's hair grew until there came a day when the Philistines thought to make a public spectacle of him before three thousand of them gathered in the temple of Dagon.

> Then Samson called to the LORD and said, "O Lord GOD, please remember me and please strengthen me just this time, O God, that I may at once be avenged of the Philistines for my two eyes." Samson grasped the two middle pillars on which the house rested, and braced himself against them, the one with his right hand and the other with his left. And Samson said, "Let me die with the Philistines!" And he bent with all his might so that the

house fell on the lords and all the people who were in it. So the dead whom he killed at his death were more than those whom he killed in his life.

Judges 16:28–30

At the end, therefore, Samson reclaimed what had been held in trust for him all along. The gifts and the calling of God are irrevocable.

Born in 1951, I am part of a population bubble of seventy million babies born in the years between the end of World War II and 1962, a Samson generation. God destined us to be world-changers. In His wisdom and grace God calls, gifts and empowers even those who do not know Him. These remain God's gifts even when misunderstood and misapplied. Satan creates nothing but only twists what God made.

We, therefore, began to use what God gave, twisted as we made it. On the good side, we old hippies did change the world. We marched for civil rights and won. We brought down the Jim Crow laws in the south that defined and enforced segregation. We integrated schools, colleges and workplaces. Creating entire genres that had never existed before, we revolutionized music forever. Called and gifted to be revolutionaries, we began to change the culture we had inherited from our parents. For good or ill, as we came of age we plunged America into a storm of social turmoil not seen since the Civil War.

Woodstock and the Jesus Movement

The high water mark came in 1969 when two seminal events took place—the Woodstock Festival and the birth of the Jesus Movement. Joel 2:28 says that in the last days God will pour out His Spirit on *all* flesh, not only on believers. For Christmas in 2010 my wife bought me the Woodstock movie, director's cut, on DVD. As I watched, the weight of all that we have somehow missed or lost brought me to tears as I realized the prophetic nature of so much of it.

Woodstock rather dramatically expressed the prophetic calling and creativity of a generation when between 300,000 and 500,000 of us converged on Max Yasgur's farm in New York State. For those who had or have an ear to hear, prophetic content saturated many of the songs and even the words of the Maharishi in a thick Indian accent intoning his call for America to lead spiritually, not merely materially. As silly as it sounds when we hear it today, God spoke it through an unbeliever and meant it.

Woodstock was much more than just "three days of peace and music." A week or two after the event, the defining lyrics, set to a sad and wistful melody, came through Joni Mitchell. Words like *golden* and *stardust* were used to describe us as human beings. She even cited our fallen condition under the devil's influence. She sang prophetic words as part of a prophetic generation gifted with a world-changing prophetic calling.

When the Jesus Movement took flight that same year, the anointing got holy, and we began to carry out the true purposes of our gifting and calling. Some say it began in 1967 in a coffeehouse in the Haight-Ashbury district of San Francisco, but it really took root in Costa Mesa, California, at Calvary Chapel beginning in 1968. That year Lonnie Frisbee was given charge of the mid-week service. By 1969 the movement had accelerated into full flower.

As true revolutionaries, we who got swept up in the movement adopted an air of aggression in our outreach. Fire burned in our bones and we conquered our contemporaries for Jesus with nothing more than the jawbone of an ass, driving around in VW microbuses, wearing raggedy jeans and singing songs on out-of-tune guitars. People fell all over themselves to get saved, and when they failed to line up to get saved, we went out and compelled them to come in.

Out of the Jesus Movement, as part of that wider explosion of creativity in song, came contemporary Christian music. This had never existed before. It was cutting edge in style and skill and it revolutionized the Church and its worship. Until that point all the churches sang old hymns accompanied by pianos and organs and simply missed the emerging youth culture. Even when called "of the devil" for doing it, our generation changed the entire church music scene.

Eventually hundreds of thousands, even millions, of young people repented and came to faith. Powered by that explosion of creative Christian music paralleling what was going on in the world, it suddenly became cool to be a follower of Jesus. The world called us Jesus freaks, and meant it as a compliment.

I find it interesting that like Samson, the calling card of our generation was long hair. Three times they kicked me out of high school for refusing to cut mine.

The Great Failure

God called and gifted us to change the world. He expected us to fulfill that destiny and grow in it, to lead our children in it, to pass them a destiny and purpose that would shape their lives and grow to become greater and more powerful than our own.

> "Now this is the commandment, the statutes and the judgments which the LORD your God has commanded me to teach you, that you might do them in the land where you are going over to possess it, so that you and your son and your grandson might fear the LORD your God, to keep all His statutes and His commandments which I command you."
>
> Deuteronomy 6:1–2

It should have been a three-generational vision, a burning purpose passed on as an inheritance. Instead, like Samson, we literally and figuratively cut our hair and sacrificed our strength and calling. The lusts of the world seduced us and we became powerless Baal worshipers. Self-focus, the antithesis of the cross, shaped our churches, our theology, our practice and our very lives.

As we began to serve mammon we began to sacrifice our calling for the sake of the job, the house, the car and the need to make money to pay for it all. As we began to develop teachings that told us how to be healthy, wealthy and successful, we lost the vision of the cross, sacrifice, selflessness and laid down love, calling it all "Christian." It was not.

Having laid down our calling and our gifts, we ceased to be world changers and fell asleep on Delilah's knee. There the curse came upon us just as it did on Samson and we became blind, lost, weak and imprisoned. No longer did we speak of conquering the world and changing it for Jesus. Our life focus had shifted.

As a result, our marriages failed at the same rate as those in the world. As a generation we fell into depression, and anti-depressants became the most prescribed medications in the Western world. Never in the history of the Western world have so many sought counseling and therapy. The most popular teachings in Christian circles became physical healing, inner healing, marriage classes, personal prophecy and the like. We sought these remedial revelations in order to ease our pain and satisfy our obsession with self, but inevitably, our disappointment grew. We should have been winning the lost and conquering the world.

As we grew ever more disappointed and disillusioned, our churches stopped growing and we began to leave organized Christianity in droves, wondering where our sense of the Lord had gone. The prophetic movement emerged, but instead of doing what God had always intended the prophetic movement to do—to equip and motivate the Body of Christ for ministry and to plant and release power for change—it catered to our self-obsession. So instead of fulfilling God's intention, we lined up to get personal words because we wanted to hear that a great destiny lay before us and we knew instinctively that we had lost our way. I called it "sanctified fortune-telling."

A Lost Generation

Instead of passing our children the heritage of a revolutionary mission, a purpose burning in our hearts as it did in our youth, we passed them purposelessness in a gilded cage of nice homes, TVs and cars. Now they pay the price as we wander in circles, chained to the grinding wheel in our blindness. A whole generation of our children stands on the brink of being lost. I admonish older believers not to think that what they see in the young people gathered in passion at the International House of Prayer in Kansas City or the School of Supernatural Ministry at Bethel Church in Redding, California, characterizes a generation. These represent isolated and unique concentrations of a small remnant. Overall, statistics tell us that we are losing a generation.

They hurt. They cut themselves. Largely abandoned, they have no other way to express their pain. They drink and abuse drugs under no delusions that it will expand their minds as we older users so naïvely thought. They do it because they have no hope. High schools in my city of Denver graduate only 30 to 40 percent of their students, and I suspect that these figures would hold across a wide spectrum of major cities in America. Many high school graduates can barely read and write. Between 75 and 80 percent of those raised in church will leave after high school and never return because what they see is a lot of old people passionlessly going through the motions and they want something raw and real. We lose them because we failed them.

The Good News of Recovery

Hear the good news! It is not over. God has not changed His mind about us as a generation. As He did with Samson, He will return our strength and restore us to our calling. We need only repent and make the right choices. If we will respond, then like the bursting of a dam we will reclaim what we laid down in greater strength than at the beginning and it will release power upon our children and upon our grandchildren. The heritage we failed to pass to them will flow once more and we will rise up, "you and your son and your grandson" (Deuteronomy 6:2), going out as a mighty army to win and change the world as we were always called to do.

We still have it in our generational soul, written into our DNA. We need only remember and respond. The generations will be healed in purpose and we together will win more souls, drive out more demons, work more wonders and take more territory in our latter years than in all our lives before, just like Samson in the temple of Dagon.

We will see our children rise higher in the things of God than we did because we will have passed them a destiny to build upon. Look for truly intergenerational churches to rise to prominence in the midst of the difficult years to come. Wedded to the prayer movement, the seed was planted in the late 1990s with the birth of IHOP and various schools of ministry that drew the young. Expect a noticeable acceleration of such truly intergenerational congregations, especially into 2013 and beyond. It will not be a sweeping culture-wide phenomenon as was the Jesus Movement, but it will result in a proliferation of lighthouse churches reaping a harvest of souls and ministering in the supernatural with a clear intergenerational demographic.

In light of this, there has never been a more urgent need for fathers and mothers in Christ to reach out to a lost generation. This generation longs for relationship, for truth, for integrity, for love and for purpose. It will be the fulfillment of Malachi 4:5–6:

"Behold, I am going to send you Elijah the prophet before the coming of the great and terrible day of the LORD. He will restore the hearts of the fathers to their children and the hearts of the children to their fathers, so that I will not come and smite the land with a curse."

We boomers must change. It is not the responsibility of the young to build a bridge to us, but rather for us to build a bridge to them. Malachi 4:5–6 begins with the restoration of the fathers' hearts to the children, not the other way around. Only thus can we stand united around the purpose in the calling and gifting of God concerning which He has never changed His mind. Together we will become a single generation of cultural and spiritual revolutionaries made up of both young and old. In so doing, we will prepare the way for the Lord's soon return as a healed bride "having no spot or wrinkle" (Ephesians 5:27).

Revolutionaries refuse to be told no. Like Samson, we of the older generation must recover what we laid down—that which God never revoked—and pursue it with perseverance and aggression. Those who respond to this call will do more damage to the kingdom of darkness in our latter years than in all our lives before. We must begin by renouncing the culture of self in all its manifestations and reclaiming the self-sacrificial life of the cross.

Now we shift the paradigm from Samson to Joshua and Caleb.

Forty Years of Wilderness at an End

In 2009 we saw the fortieth anniversary of the Woodstock Festival and the acceleration of the Jesus Movement. As a chosen generation we figuratively left slavery in Egypt to begin a journey to the Promised Land. In that first Exodus, Israel rejected their calling, refused to have faith and chose not to root out idolatry from their hearts. Consequently, for forty years they wandered in the dry places of the desert. In spite of several pulses of renewal that came and went, so did we.

Over the span of four decades after the Exodus from Egypt the Lord waited until the faithless among the people of Israel had died off and only Joshua and Caleb of that first generation remained. Out of hundreds of thousands, those two men alone stood out as those who had chosen faith, passion and strength in the service of the Lord. Caleb declared,

> "Now behold, the LORD has let me live, just as He spoke, these forty-five years, from the time that the LORD spoke this word to Moses, when Israel walked in the wilderness; and now behold, I am eighty-five years old today. I am still as strong today as I was in the day Moses sent me; as my strength was then, so my strength is now, for war and for going out and coming in."
>
> Joshua 14:10–11

As Joshua and Caleb led the people, the next generation, into the land of promise, they passed a destiny and a purpose to the young, and together they took the Promised Land.

In 2009, the fortieth year after Woodstock and the release of the Jesus Movement, something shifted in the Spirit. The student awakening at the International House of Prayer began that year, birthed out of the prayer movement that IHOP stands for and illustrating the power of the kind of prayer offered in Revelation 8 that saw the angel cast fire into the earth. This is the season for heaven-magnified intercession. The fire is falling!

The student awakening at IHOP was no accident of history, but a deliberate move of God who loves to play with numbers. For forty literal years we have seen a slow dying off of the generation that came out of Egypt into freedom through the Jesus Movement. Unfortunately, that generation as a whole failed to transcend the culture of self to take the promised land of destiny to which God had called them. A great many have therefore died along the way, some literally and many more spiritually, casualties of the worship of Baal and the loss of hope and faith that results from it.

Now the Promised Land lies before us, the fulfillment of the destiny prophesied for us more than forty years ago. God stands ready to loose an outpouring of the Spirit not seen since Pentecost for its power and impact. A Samson generation, a remnant of Joshuas and Calebs, now arises to lead a second and third generation in passion to a great destiny in these last days before the return of the Lord. These have become world-changers once more because they never stopped and never allowed their passion to recede.

Some few will be names we recognize. Bill Johnson at Bethel Church in Redding, California, Mike Bickle at the International House of Prayer in Kansas City and John Arnott of Catch the Fire Ministries stand out as forerunners. Many more will be nameless and faceless, humbly fulfilling their callings in local churches in hidden places. Together these constitute a vital remnant who have stayed the course and chosen not to allow their strength to diminish in the service of the Lord as the years have passed.

A new season of victory and anointing lies before us. A fresh manifestation of God's Spirit looms just around the corner, bathed in the Father's love and infused with its power. Like the hairs that stand up on our bodies in the presence of an electric current, we can already feel its nearness. The critics will try to stop it, speaking slanderously of those of us who welcome this move and walk in it, but it cannot and will not be stopped. It is the last days outpouring and it can only happen as the young and the old dance together, reconciled in heart, in love and in purpose.

The Choice for Passion and Connection

Who are the Joshuas and the Calebs among us? Who will recover a prophetic destiny for a generation? Who among us will stand

189

to the calling? The answer begins with a determination to repent for the lost years, for abandoning our children to our own self-focus. It begins with a broken heart. As I reached out to my own adult son, alienated from me during my years of burnout and consequent emotional turmoil, I knelt before him, asked his forgiveness, both of us in tears, and swore, "I will never not be there for you ever again." I have kept my word.

Today he serves as my co-pastor, exercising a greater anointing than my own, respected as a leader of both young and old, and from the two of us in unity and partnership flows an anointing much stronger than the mere sum of our parts. The hearts of the fathers must be restored to the children and the children to the fathers and then the "great and terrible day of LORD" will come with the return of Jesus (Malachi 4:5).

There will, therefore, never be another revival affecting only a single generation. In the Body of Christ, among the sons and daughters of God, the generations will stand together, receiving together and conquering for the Gospel together or there will be nothing at all.

> "Then the virgin will rejoice in the dance, and the young men and the old, together, for I will turn their mourning into joy and will comfort them and give them joy for their sorrow. I will fill the soul of the priests with abundance, and My people will be satisfied with My goodness," declares the LORD.
>
> Jeremiah 31:13–14

I confess that I have grown weary of spending much of my time with a bunch of middle-aged men and women trying to relive some past move of God or simply trying to get by in their faith, self-absorbed, disillusioned, always depressed and half asleep spiritually. The glory cloud has moved and continues to move. We must change and move with it, even if only a remnant of the Woodstock generation chooses to take that road with us.

We must walk with this last days generation of passionate young people and lift them up to lead alongside us in partnership. The Lord will not return before He brings this prophetic word to pass among His people (see Malachi 4:5–6).

The time is now. A people of true greatness must, and will, arise in the midst of the coming storm to bring in a harvest of souls with signs, wonders and the raw presence of God unprecedented in the history of our faith. It has already begun, but a part of it will be some of the most dramatic and numerous demonic deliverances many of us have ever seen. More to come in the following chapter.

14

REVELATION EVENTS
FORESHADOWED

I realize that interpretations of the book of Revelation vary widely and draw volumes of debate. I have no intention of introducing that debate into the content of this book. That being said, I do believe as most do, that some things speak clearly to the days immediately ahead of us. Ultimately, according to Revelation, events more dire than those I predict in this book must occur before all is fulfilled and the end comes. In this book I speak primarily to the season just before us, the time remaining between now and the events of the end.

I suggest that most future events of eschatological significance are almost always preceded by foreshadowing in the present. The future Kingdom of God, for instance, shines in upon us now, and the powers of the age to come have invaded the time in which we now live, at least in part. Were this not the case, we would see no signs, wonders, healings or deliverances. The same is true of many of the dire biblical prophecies of the last days. As the time of fulfillment approaches, we see foreshadowing of the fullness to come, both in natural events and in demonic afflictions.

Effects in Nature

Both Matthew 24 and Revelation 7 and 8 predict natural disasters resulting in apocalyptic shortages of essential goods and services in the days leading up to the return of the Lord. It would be difficult not to conclude that John saw the effects of the erosion of the ozone layer now under way eventually destroying green and growing things and that in chapter 8 he witnessed objects entering the atmosphere and crashing into the sea and the land to destroy vast swaths of life, vegetation and sustenance for humankind.

As we have moved nearer to the time foreseen by John, we have already witnessed an escalation of catastrophic events. The spring of 2011 saw a record number of tornadoes strike the heartland of America with unprecedented levels of power and destruction to major population areas. August 2011 saw an epochal hurricane rake the east coast, causing billions of dollars in damage and affecting more people than any storm in U.S. history. Anyone reading the news knows how widespread these sorts of catastrophes have been.

As climate change accelerates, with or without the impact of a celestial body, agriculture will suffer and world hunger will increase. Revelation predicts such food shortages on a massive scale. Already China's breadbasket rice-growing region labors under an extended drought, as does the state of Texas in the U.S., now declared a disaster area, and parts of the South. In years to come we will see acceleration of what John prophesied.

The earthquake that struck Japan moved that nation as much as eight feet and spawned an enormous tidal wave that killed thousands and devastated vast swaths of land. Volcanoes have been erupting. As I write in the summer of 2011 massive wild-fires have scorched record-setting tracts of land in the American West. According to a news article published on June 21, 2011, over Yahoo's online news agency (headline: "Ocean life on the brink of mass extinctions: study") and echoed in many other places, our seas are in danger or in the process of suffering mass extinctions of wildlife at a magnitude not seen at any other time in earth's history. Revelation prophesies the death of one-third of living things in the sea, while today one sixth of the earth's population relies on fish for primary dietary protein intake. These things will accelerate as the time of fulfillment approaches.

These represent just a few of the devastating natural events of recent years. In the first six months of 2011 the world suffered more devastating natural disasters than in the entirety of any prior year on record. While I will refrain from trying to predict specifically where coming disasters will strike, I state categorically that there will be many disruptive events in more and more places as this five-year period of grace to prepare begins to expire. I fear especially for the American Midwest, both American coasts, anywhere in the Pacific or bordering on it, Europe and Asia.

Crop failures brought on by these disasters will result in higher prices for food as demand for relief in the form of food and other goods and services collides with dwindling supply. Already we see this upward trend. This, in turn, will strain the world's welfare agencies and emergency response organizations in terms of finances and other resources. As a result, many regions of the world will be left to fend for themselves as best they can while human suffering grows.

The Coming Increase in Demonic Activity

Most commentators agree that the swarm of locusts released from the abyss in Revelation 9 in the final days leading to the

Lord's return symbolizes a demonic horde set loose upon the earth to afflict those who have not been marked as belonging to the Lord. As previously stated, such coming events are often preceded by foreshadowing that can be felt and observed in the here and now, especially as the time of fulfillment draws nearer.

God's laws describe the operational dynamic of the universe, the way things actually work. He gave us these laws to ensure that we would live well. When these laws are violated, destruction comes, initially not so much because of God's wrath but as the result of natural law. Sin brings forth death (see James 1:15). This is nothing more than universal natural law operating in the same immutable manner as the natural laws of gravity or inertia. Unhappiness, disintegration of the family, broken lives and, ultimately, societal disintegration result.

Sin not only destroys by means of natural consequence, it also opens the door to demonic oppression and the consequent magnification of sin's destructive effects. Another more devastating consequence of sin, therefore, will soon break upon us in a rising wave of human suffering. I see coming the vanguard of the Revelation 9 demonic horde afflicting mankind. For several decades this has been building up in a kind of stealth mode, nearly hidden beneath the surface, while sin, and the acceptance of sin, has visibly accelerated. It has been, as it were, a covert infiltration allowing the people of the world to believe that they remain in control of their lives even as basic biblical morality has been openly discarded. This concealment must soon end as the enemy's long preparation erupts into a full and open manifestation of out-of-control destruction.

Very soon now we will see a dramatic rise in demonic manifestation and oppression. Practitioners of psychology and medicine will diagnose it as mental illness but will not be able to explain the increase. Unable to discern the true cause, they will try to control the growing insanity through medication.

At the less extreme end, more and more people will find themselves dealing with unprecedented depths of depression, addiction and obsession. Divorce rates will increase, as will pregnancies out of wedlock. Sexual abuse of both children and adults has already been on the rise, but expect significant increases in the days to come. These things will be demonically driven. Ministries that understand demonization will find themselves much more engaged in deliverance ministry than at any previous time. Healing ministries must prepare and train now for the onslaught.

In short, sin and delusion will be more openly energized by demonic forces. I believe that many of us in healing ministries will begin to see this rise in demonic manifestations even before this book can be released.

Here are some specific causes.

Drug Abuse

By studying the dynamics of Israel's demise in the Old Testament and the behavior that the demonic gods of the nations inspired in Israel, we see that the demonic world delights in idolatry, false doctrines, inaccurate assumptions about God, self-focus, sexual compromise, sexual perversion and child abuse. Secondary issues involve drug abuse of various kinds. Alcohol was the only drug these ancient people knew. Scripture therefore speaks strongly to the general issue of the destruction wrought through intoxication. It makes no difference which drug exerts the influence, the effect of intoxication on life and spirituality remains.

While alcohol abuse and its destructive effects on life, spirituality and relationships have always been apparent, some drugs have a particularly strong effect in opening the human psyche to demonic influence. The list of available intoxicants seems to grow with every passing year, but among those with the strongest spiritual consequences are marijuana, peyote, mescaline and similar substances. A number of these have been used in traditional Native American ceremonies (and other tribal societies) because of their effectiveness in removing the veil between the physical world and the spiritual realm.

In the same way that not all that glitters is gold, however, not all that seems spiritual is God. God forbids intoxication for good reason. No matter what drug we use to induce an altered state of consciousness, it remains intoxication, a counterfeit and a lie. This inhibits true spirituality and opens the user to demonic influence as the normal safeguards against demonic invasion are suppressed or removed.

The current culture of marijuana use and its increasing acceptance as a so-called harmless drug are of particular concern. An entire generation is being demonically conditioned for an enormous demonic invasion. Behind the growing delusion regarding its acceptability and the denial of its negative effects is a principality-level demonic entity manipulating the thoughts and feelings of a huge segment of our culture. As a result, when you challenge the delusions sown through the influence of this principality, you meet with the kind of angry intensity and offense you encounter when someone's religion is attacked and they react to defend it. I find this to be an unmistakable sign of idolatrous demonic influence.

Satan was a liar from the beginning and this lie is a big one. Far from harmless, the marijuana plague not only presents many physical dangers proven through research denied or ignored by the marijuana culture. More important, it opens its users to slow and steady demonic oppression of spirituality, emotional life and healthy relationships. We have not yet seen the full magnitude of destruction to come from just this one drug among many—with the emphasis on "many"—but we will, and soon.

Sexual Compromise

I estimate that in 35 years of full-time professional ministry I have performed between 200 and 300 weddings. Of this number, I can still count on the fingers of my two hands the number of couples who came to their wedding night as virgins, at least to one another. Over the last couple of years the problem has worsened. I have been performing increasing numbers of weddings for couples who have lived together for several years and borne children without benefit of marriage. Happy and honored to make it right before God, I mean no condemnation. This does, however, highlight a growing epidemic of sexual compromise, even in the Church, not to mention the compromises being exposed in major national leaders, both in the Church and the secular world.

Addiction to pornography captivates an astonishing number of men, including a huge percentage of clergy. One in three women will be sexually molested or raped during her lifetime. Among the young, the problem grows worse. My son, the youth pastor, tells me that a near majority of teenage girls coming into our youth group have at some point been molested by a father, a stepfather, mom's boyfriend, a brother, an uncle or some other person.

Having been passed little or no foundation in spirituality or morality by their self-absorbed parents, we see growing numbers of teenage girls and young women choosing pregnancy out of wedlock. Often, they announce their pregnancies to us with joy, expecting congratulations. We love their babies, but we cannot be happy for the tragedies that will unfold over many years as a result of these poor choices made for self-centered reasons.

In the context of warning the believers in Corinth, the apostle Paul wrote,

> On the contrary, you yourselves wrong and defraud. You do this even to your brethren. Or do you not know that the unrighteous

will not inherit the kingdom of God? Do not be deceived; neither fornicators, nor idolaters, nor adulterers, nor effeminate, nor homosexuals, nor thieves, nor the covetous, nor drunkards, nor revilers, nor swindlers, will inherit the kingdom of God.

1 Corinthians 6:8–10

Four items in this list directly address the issue of sexual sin and a fifth, idolatry, likely includes the orgies that often accompanied pagan worship in the Roman world.

"The unrighteous will not inherit the Kingdom of God." Clearly, a deliberately chosen lifestyle of sin can endanger one's salvation. The popular doctrine of eternal security, with which I take issue, does not help. This being true, we must understand that sexual sin, more than many other kinds of sin, opens one up to demonic oppression and obsession. Witness the upsurge in child sexual abuse, rape and pornography we have seen in recent decades. In days to come it will become increasingly apparent that sexual perversion and violence are being driven out of control by demonic influences. Increasing numbers of lives will be destroyed. Marriages will break up. Children will be defiled and abused.

Early in my career, I was an Elijah House counselor full time. Since then I have kept touch with the counseling world. In all that time, never have I seen a case of sexual abuse in which demonic influence was not present to drive the perpetrator and often to visit a lifetime of defilement upon the victim until deliverance and healing put a stop to it. In coming years we will see a significant escalation of sexual perversion, violation and violence. Simple counseling and healing ministry will not suffice to heal many of those affected by this scourge. Deliverance will be required. Repentance must be included in any genuine or lasting deliverance, but many will be so trapped in the grip of demonic influence, delusion and denial they will be unable to repent. Demonic blinders will have effectively rendered them unable to see their behavior as sinful or wrong and destruction will therefore continue in and through them. "Therefore God gave them over in the lusts of their hearts to impurity, so that their bodies would be dishonored among them " (Romans 1:24). Romans 1:28 is like it: "And just as they did not see fit to acknowledge God any longer, God gave them over to a depraved mind, to do those things which are not proper."

Sexual compromise is *never* a sin affecting only the one committing the trespass. Because we have been created in God's image "male and female" (see Genesis 1:27), our sexuality lies at the core of who we are in the image of God. Sexual sin, trespass and degradation, therefore, present the most tempting target for the enemy of our soul. Damaging that which is most precious to God—His image—constitutes the ultimate act of hatred in his desire to wound God. Sexual sin in just one person affects us all, and most of all, our Lord.

Doctrines of Demons

Demons commonly masquerade as angels, even posing as God Himself. According to 2 Corinthians 11:14, Satan disguises himself as an angel of light. As such, he introduces extra-biblical "revelation" to those open to receive it, presenting it as truth, often based on something the recipient has experienced. Scripture must always stand as our baseline and defense, but when we depart from sound doctrine and begin exalting personal experience or personal revelation to the level of established fact, we step beyond the boundaries set for our defense and begin to hear the voice of the demonic. That voice might sound like God, but the end is shipwreck of faith, life and ministry.

Demonic delusion and erosion of core doctrines will, therefore, multiply in the coming years until essential and genuine Christianity becomes more and more difficult to find. Already we see the rise of "Chrislam," an amalgam of Christianity and

Islam predicated on the erroneous assumption that each of these faiths worships the same God. Many we once regarded as solidly evangelical have begun to compromise and cooperate with the demon who calls himself Allah.

I certainly do not advocate avoiding Muslims as people or engaging in any sort of hatred. We must meet them with the Father's love, but this does not and must not include sharing pulpits, worship services or buildings. Allah is a demon, a ruling principality pretending to be God.

The "abomination of desolation" mentioned in Matthew 24:15 references the prophecy of Daniel 11:31, which saw fulfillment circa 168 B.C. when the Greek ruler Antiochus Epiphanes set up an idol of Zeus in the Jerusalem Temple and sacrificed a pig on the altar. I suggest that allowing servants of the demon Allah to speak in our churches, affirming Allah as the same God we worship and compromising with other religions in similar ways qualifies as a fulfillment of the prophecy in Matthew 24:15 presaging the end times. Expect this movement of "reconciliation" to grow. It will be demonically inspired and tempting in the extreme, posing as tolerance, peace and love, but the consequences will ultimately destroy those who participate.

Expect a growing trend of ungodly syncretism to invade the Church, especially as many whom we once regarded as Bible-believing pastors and churches adopt universalism and the idea that there is no hell. This opens the door to cooperation with faiths that have nothing in common with Christianity.

The Move of God

The New Testament record shows that whenever the Kingdom of God begins to move and to affect the course of human lives, truly penetrating the heart, we see a corresponding increase in demonic activity. Witness how frequently Jesus addressed demonic possession and oppression. The very presence of God stirs up the demonic. As John Arnott has put it, "When the good comes in the bad comes out," and it frequently comes out screaming. The Spirit of God does not bring the demonic, but rather upsets what is already present in order to dislodge the unclean influence.

Those who welcome the cleansing will be delivered and set free. Those who resist and cling to their sin will exhibit a growing contempt for all things Christian as the Holy Spirit resident in believers confronts demonic influence and inspires demonic hatred. Humans coming under this influence and acting it out will believe themselves to be acting on their own volition, even standing for justice. Under the guise of "love," they will embrace ungodly beliefs and practices, but they will be acting on demonic inspiration. Increasingly, men and women will call good evil and evil good (see Isaiah 5:20) to their own harm and will hate those who cannot agree with them.

Incurable Disease

Revelation 6, 8 and 9 all include prophecies of devastating disease. Already we see an increase in bacteria that have developed immunity to antibiotics. The emergence of AIDS as a sexually transmitted disease should have been an alarm bell alerting us to the development of viruses for which we know no cure. As the time of the fulfillment of the prophecies in Revelation approaches, the world will see an increase in viral mutations and other forms of illness for which medical science has no answers.

In the United States the promise of Obamacare, if not repealed, will be exposed as a lie. It will not make medical care more accessible, but will have the opposite effect as millions more people pour into a system already strained by too few general practitioners. Fewer young people will aspire to be doctors because the profession will hold less monetary appeal than it does now. In any case, the coming increase in potentially deadly disease will strain medical systems and resources.

At such times, God ramps up Kingdom power through His people, pouring out His Spirit to minister miraculously. Genuine healing ministries—not the showy charlatans we have seen through the years—will multiply. Already in many places the average layperson has learned that he or she can minister God's love and compassion in this kind of demonstration of power. The age of the Body of Christ has come. The time of the great healing evangelist doing it all *for* us has ended. Ordinary people will carry God's healing to the workplace, the neighborhood and, yes, into our regular church services just as Jesus and the disciples did so long ago. Wise ministries will prepare for this, pray for and train for this.

Conclusion

The years that lie before us may be difficult ones, but they are mere precursors to the more dire events of the apocalypse to come before the Lord's return. We will experience increasing foreshadowing of end time events in the years before these events actually unfold. These will manifest on both the natural and supernatural planes. We have time yet to prepare ourselves as believers. We must use this time wisely and get ready both to stand the ground and to minister in love.

PART III

SHORT
THEMES

15

ISLAM

Christian fear of Islam in the face of growing immigration by Islamic people into Western countries is misplaced. Those who carry such fear have frankly lost faith in the compelling power of the Gospel. "Be of sober spirit, be on the alert. Your adversary, the devil, prowls around like a roaring lion, seeking someone to devour" (1 Peter 5:8). He is only "like" a roaring lion, a pretender putting up a front, but he is not a real lion; or did we forget that Jesus utterly defeated him when He died on the cross and rose from the dead? Rotten at its core, Islam will fall despite its outward appearance of strength.

The Coming Judgment

Predominantly Islamic nations will soon suffer judgment, especially those that support Sharia law and its cruelties. The Arab spring of 2011 was only the beginning, the first of many cracks that must eventually widen into chasms. Some time ago, the Lord told me that, having no real concept of the Father's love,

Islam would ultimately collapse under the weight of its own lovelessness. This does not mean that it will cease to exist, but rather that its influence in the world will begin to wane in the face of a set of influences including, but not exclusive to, the advance of Christianity.

In the long term, the judgment on Islamic nations and governments will come partly in the form of diminishing wealth. This will unfold as an energy revolution gathers strength that will gradually transition us out of an oil-dominated culture and economy. Other forms of energy will displace oil as the predominant fuel. Eventually, a whole new economy will be birthed.

As prosperity comes to Islamic immigrants in the world outside traditionally Muslim countries, the power of Islam in their lives will diminish. Historically, radical religion of any kind has always thrived under conditions of poverty and has lost power in the face of wealth. The promise of a better life economically, not religion or some sense of Islamic evangelistic fervor, is the force driving Islamic people to immigrate to Western nations. Prosperity erodes religious fervor as people come to rely on and find comfort in things rather than religion.

God's Strategy

Because many Islamic nations have outlawed the practice of Christianity or severely limited any form of evangelistic activity, making it difficult for us to go to them, God has brought Muslim people to us through immigration. Quite apart from any danger presented by growing Muslim populations in nominally Christian nations, we who understand the power of the Kingdom of God have been presented with an opportunity and a mission, a God-breathed strategy for the salvation of millions.

For example, a Spirit-filled church in a Scandinavian country saw that Muslim refugees from repressive Islamic nations were being housed in government facilities near them. Realizing that these people had been deprived of their ethnic culture by the imposition of radical Islamic law, the church decided to reach out with cultural events.

Today they invite Muslims to celebrations of culture in which their native music, dance and culinary arts that have been denied them in their own nations can be shared. Toward the end of each evening, the church asks to share its own Christian culture. The worship band then takes the stage and begins to praise God. As the Holy Spirit fills the room, people begin to feel the touch of God; and when dramatic, miraculous healings begin to manifest, the gathered soon-to-be Christians start asking questions. Having experienced both the Father's love and the power of the Kingdom of God, many of these Muslims become believers in Jesus and then eventually return to their native countries to start covert house churches.

As a strategy for reaching Muslim people, God has positioned Kingdom congregations, lighthouse churches like those I described in chapter 5, in the nations to which they have immigrated. We need not and must not be afraid of this influx of people Jesus died to save, but rather believe in and act on the power of what we have been given.

This is clearly a conditional prophetic word; it depends on the choices we believers make. I merely point out the strategy of God, the power of our witness and His intention to reach a people group. Is Islamic expansion an attack or a God-given opportunity? Is it a danger to us or has God presented us with a blessing? Would God really want to leave an entire people group locked away from the opportunity to hear the Gospel of salvation just to keep safe those of us who already believe?

If we will lay aside our fears and pick up our authority in the Lord as God intends, millions will be saved.

As I write, I have just received the latest issue of *Charisma Magazine*. Included in it are reports of exponential increases in Christian populations in closed Muslim nations as well as testimonies from former Muslims claiming that Jesus appeared to them in person to bring about their conversion. I rest my case.

16

A NEW JEWISH EXODUS

> For I do not want you, brethren, to be uninformed of this mystery—so that you will not be wise in your own estimation—that a partial hardening has happened to Israel until the fullness of the Gentiles has come in; and so all Israel will be saved; just as it is written, "The Deliverer will come from Zion, He will remove ungodliness from Jacob."
>
> Romans 11:25–26

In the symbolism of the ministry of the two witnesses in Revelation 11, we see the eventual conversion of the Jews, a new Jewish exodus from an ancient form of slavery, just as Paul foresaw it in Romans 11. According to the first two chapters of Revelation, lampstands stand for churches. The two witnesses—two lampstands, according to Revelation 11:4—must therefore symbolize the end time restoration and magnified witness of the two halves of the Body of Christ in a restored balance.

The Two Halves

The early Church consisted of two parts—Messianic synagogues made up of Jews who knew Jesus as their Messiah, and Gentile churches grafted in by grace. Eventually the Messianic church died out and nearly two millennia of ugly relations between Jews and Gentiles followed, but that time is coming to an end. This points to the fulfillment of Paul's prophecy that the Jewish people as a whole would one day be grafted back into the trunk of their own olive tree. Now is the time for that prophecy to be fulfilled.

Without debating the merits of various interpretations of Luke 21:24, which says that "Jerusalem will be trampled under foot by the Gentiles until the times of the Gentiles are fulfilled," I suggest that it refers to the time when exclusive domination of Christian faith by Gentiles ends and Jewish people come to know their Messiah *en masse*. While those who resist will always be with us, we will nevertheless see a breakthrough among Jewish people, both in Israel and in other parts of the world. The revelation of Jesus' true identity will break upon the descendants of Abraham, Isaac and Jacob, and their inclusion, the completion of their true ancestral faith, will deeply enrich us all, just as Paul said it would.

The Current Reality

Early in 2011, I had the privilege of sharing lunch with a Messianic rabbi from Israel. Having come to the United States to study at a seminary in New York, he took time to pay us a brief visit in Denver. He told me that a decade ago there were just 24 Messianic synagogues in Israel, but that today that number has grown to some 240, mostly pastored by Jewish believers who came to the Lord during the Jesus Movement of the '60s and '70s. Here we find yet another parallel to the forty-year paradigm of the exodus from slavery, the wilderness sojourn and the entrance into the Promised Land. It began in micro-cosm circa 1969 and now, around the forty-year mark, it has gathered strength through Joshuas and Calebs who have stood their ground during the wilderness years.

Messianic synagogues have multiplied in the United States and other nations as well. Merely the beginning of a movement, this groundswell will gain strength over the next ten years as part of the prophesied complex of events leading up to the return of the Lord.

17

THE LOOMING THREAT OF WAR

Especially in light of the current historic recession, war remains a significant danger with numerous flash points around the world. Pray for strength and wisdom for our leaders and for the Lord to disarm the spirit of war. Historically, the enemy has often incited war to stop a worldwide revival. In 1904, the great Welsh Revival resulted in waves of young missionaries going out into the world. In 1906, the Azusa Street Revival broke out and ignited the Pentecostal Movement, and again missions flowered. People affected by those revivals talked seriously of being able to complete the Great Commission within their lifetimes and then the Lord would come in accord with Matthew 24:14, "This gospel of the kingdom shall be preached in the whole world as a testimony to all the nations, and then the end will come."

In 1914, the enemy of our soul ignited World War I and put an end to that missions thrust by neutralizing the generation drafted to fight the war. World War II grew out of the Great Depression and again took out a generation. The Jesus Movement sprang up in the late 1960s and early 1970s as hundreds of thousands of young people came to Jesus. The Vietnam War, coupled with the culture of self, however, largely neutralized the Jesus Movement in America before it could have its full impact.

Once more, we stand on the cusp. Unprecedented worldwide revival is under way. Large numbers of people are coming to Jesus on every continent. The enemy would love to start a war to shut it all down before the current younger generation in the Western world can experience a revival in their own time—something they have yet to see in fullness.

Prayer, not diplomacy, will head off war, but in any call for prayer we must rise above our own personal concerns, in which the current demon-inspired blanket of fear imprisons us, and choose to focus on issues larger and more significant than our own individual lives. Do this, and the sons and daughters of God will prevail.

18

MORE ON AMERICA

One need not be prophetic to know that something has dramatically changed in America. What may not be so obvious is what it means to us and how we must respond.

Shattered National Consciousness

Despite a quickening stream of prophecies to the contrary, the United States will not disintegrate or break up. The center of our national identity will fragment, however. This is already in evidence and has progressed to the point that it cannot be stopped. Historically, incoming immigrants have always been eager to become Americans in both language and culture, but no longer. Preferring to create their own cultural and linguistic islands, incoming ethnic groups will be less and less inclined to become cultural Americans.

This kind of diversity will shatter the centered national identity we once knew. As a result, politics will become increasingly splintered and we will find it more and more difficult to come

216

to any form of national unity. Racial and ethnic differences will lead to escalating tensions as we discover what European leaders already know—that multiculturalism does not work and that nations can only survive and thrive with a centered national consciousness. Some among us have seen and sensed this looming fragmentation and have misinterpreted it as the imminent breakup of the nation, but the essence of it will be ethnic and racial. Ultimately these tensions will escalate into violence as one group claims discrimination by another and as economic disparities between people groups grow larger.

Churches like my own congregation will be called to stand in the gap. I do not foresee a great number of multicultural churches springing up. Immigrants coming into the country now generally reject that, again preferring to assemble with people of their own culture with whom they can identify and feel comfortable. Certain lighthouse churches, however, can and will model interracial harmony in their midst. These can and will speak prophetically into conflicts as they develop and as they are able.

The Right versus the Left

The fight between the right and the left will continue to intensify. As I write, Congress has just come through another battle over the debt ceiling. Lawmakers temporarily averted the immediate danger, although America's credit rating suffered a downgrade. The real issue, however, was never the budget, the debt ceiling or any other item of concern as much as an ongoing philosophical battle over the direction of the country. This constitutes the root of the intransigence and increasing bitterness exhibited by both parties. Casting true logic to the winds, people defend political philosophies more vehemently than they do money, much as they defend their respective religions as one side against the other claims exclusivity on matters of truth. Make no mistake, politics and political ideology carry the force of religion in America.

For this reason, the danger remains. On this and other issues, Washington's battles and apparent paralysis will continue well into the future, Progressives versus Conservatives, neither side willing to concede anything to the other and each characterizing the opposition as evil. For the foreseeable future the debates will remain bitter and accusatory while our president appears ever more impotent to provide the leadership necessary to carry us through. Two thousand and twelve will bring a burst of hope and the promise of change, but it will not last.

In writing this, I am not being political, but am rather pointing out the deeply divided condition of the nation. Divisions range from politics to religion to race. Not since the Civil War have we seen so many fractures in so many places at such deep levels. We are no longer "one nation" and no longer does our nation regard itself to be "under God" in any effective sense. The bad news is that we are beyond healing. Certain trends have been allowed to go too far unchecked and we now live with a shattered national consciousness, a downgraded consciousness of morality and a broken sense of who we are as a people.

A Change of Strategy

This situation requires a change of strategy on the part of Christians. We cannot make America what it once was and we need to stop wasting our efforts trying. We can make no impact on the future by looking to the past. The America many of us grew up in and came to love is gone forever. We must therefore surrender our bitterness and anger over this state of affairs, alter course and deal with the situation as it is, rather than as we believe it once was or how we would like it to be. Strategies shift as realities shift. We must therefore learn from the early Christians living under Roman domination because this increasingly is the situation in which we find ourselves. (See Romans 8 and 10.)

In light of so much that I have said in this book, I have long since surrendered the idea that we are a Christian nation or that we will return to any kind of admission that we were ever such. I refuse to debate whether there ever was a time when we truly were Christian. What is important is that my nation, my true citizenship, is the Church of Jesus Christ and I will direct my prophetic cries to her heart. She is black, white, brown and Asian, Chinese, Japanese, Caucasian and Slavic, to mention a few. I cannot and will not confuse my loyalties by making my love of America a point of faith.

Use your vote in the coming days to express your conscience in the political realm but invest your truest effort in strengthening the Lord's Bride and bringing about her health. This is the struggle we can win. The storm approaches, icebergs lie ahead, the *Titanic* will sink because no one has the power to turn the ship. And we, the Church, must be ready with lifeboats and supplies, healers and lovers with lights to dispel the darkness and rescue those who will be drowning as the ship founders.

I have written that it will not be as bad as many claim, but it will certainly be bad enough. For us who have prepared our churches and ourselves effectively, the days to come will be filled with glory as God increases His acts of mercy, His demonstrations of power and His love through us who will step forward boldly and with passion. This is our time to rise and shine, not to join the world in fear and depression. The people of the world will suffer as increasing sin bears its inevitable fruit of destruction. Many will cry out to be saved. We must be ready.

Let the "sons of God" who have absorbed His nature and character (see Romans 8:28–29) arise at last as the earth suffers the birth pangs of the coming Kingdom of God.

R. Loren Sandford grew up a preacher's son in the Congregational Church in Illinois, Kansas and north Idaho. As a teenager he played rock music professionally over three states and two provinces of Canada before leaving to attend the College of Idaho. In 1973, he completed a B.A. degree in music education, then moved to California and attended Fuller Theological Seminary in Pasadena, earning a Master's of Divinity degree in 1976.

Since 1976, Loren has served four churches full-time, successfully planting two of them himself, including New Song Church and Ministries, Denver, Colorado, where he remains the senior pastor. In 1979 and 1980, he co-directed Elijah House (an international ministry in Christian counseling and counselor training) and continues to be in demand internationally, primarily for teaching but also for leading worship. Initially ordained in a mainline denomination where he served on the national board for the charismatic renewal group within that affiliation, he has since served in the Vineyard (1988–92) and since 1996 has been affiliated with Partners in Harvest, a new association of churches associated with the Toronto Airport Christian Fellowship (now known as Catch the Fire Toronto) and the renewal centered there. He has been a member of the International Input Council for Partners in Harvest, oversees the central western region for that family of churches and is a recognized prophetic voice within the movement.

In 1991, he was the worship leader for the first Promise Keepers mass men's meeting at the CU Event Center in Boulder,

Colorado, and has released fourteen CDs of original music, most of it for worship. In addition to the music, Loren is the author of *Purifying the Prophetic: Breaking Free from the Spirit of Self-Fulfillment*, *Understanding Prophetic People: Blessings and Problems with the Prophetic Gift*, *The Prophetic Church: Wielding the Power to Change the World*, *Renewal for the Wounded Warrior: A Burnout Survival Guide for Believers* and now *Visions of the Coming Days: What to Look for and How to Prepare*.

Married to Beth since 1972, they have three grown children and nine grandchildren. Loren is also a member of the Osage Nation, a Native American tribe centered in Oklahoma.